# IFIP Advances in Information and Communication Technology 669

## Editor-in-Chief

*Kai Rannenberg, Goethe University Frankfurt, Germany*

## Editorial Board Members

TC 1 – Foundations of Computer Science
  *Luís Soares Barbosa*, *University of Minho, Braga, Portugal*

TC 2 – Software: Theory and Practice
  *Michael Goedicke, University of Duisburg-Essen, Germany*

TC 3 – Education
  *Arthur Tatnall*, *Victoria University, Melbourne, Australia*

TC 5 – Information Technology Applications
  *Erich J. Neuhold, University of Vienna, Austria*

TC 6 – Communication Systems
  *Burkhard Stiller, University of Zurich, Zürich, Switzerland*

TC 7 – System Modeling and Optimization
  *Lukasz Stettner, Institute of Mathematics, Polish Academy of Sciences, Warsaw, Poland*

TC 8 – Information Systems
  *Jan Pries-Heje, Roskilde University, Denmark*

TC 9 – ICT and Society
  *David Kreps*, *National University of Ireland, Galway, Ireland*

TC 10 – Computer Systems Technology
  *Achim Rettberg, Hamm-Lippstadt University of Applied Sciences, Hamm, Germany*

TC 11 – Security and Privacy Protection in Information Processing Systems
  *Steven Furnell*, *Plymouth University, UK*

TC 12 – Artificial Intelligence
  *Eunika Mercier-Laurent*, *University of Reims Champagne-Ardenne, Reims, France*

TC 13 – Human-Computer Interaction
  *Marco Winckler*, *University of Nice Sophia Antipolis, France*

TC 14 – Entertainment Computing
  *Rainer Malaka, University of Bremen, Germany*

# IFIP Advances in Information and Communication Technology

The IFIP AICT series publishes state-of-the-art results in the sciences and technologies of information and communication. The scope of the series includes: foundations of computer science; software theory and practice; education; computer applications in technology; communication systems; systems modeling and optimization; information systems; ICT and society; computer systems technology; security and protection in information processing systems; artificial intelligence; and human-computer interaction.

Edited volumes and proceedings of refereed international conferences in computer science and interdisciplinary fields are featured. These results often precede journal publication and represent the most current research.

The principal aim of the IFIP AICT series is to encourage education and the dissemination and exchange of information about all aspects of computing.

More information about this series at https://link.springer.com/bookseries/6102

Stefan Henkler · Márcio Kreutz ·
Marco A. Wehrmeister ·
Marcelo Götz · Achim Rettberg
Editors

# Designing Modern Embedded Systems: Software, Hardware, and Applications

7th IFIP TC 10 International
Embedded Systems Symposium, IESS 2022
Lippstadt, Germany, November 3–4, 2022
Proceedings

Springer

*Editors*
Stefan Henkler
Hamm-Lippstadt University of Applied
Sciences
Hamm, Germany

Márcio Kreutz 🆔
Federal University of Rio Grande do Norte
Natal, Rio Grande do Norte, Brazil

Marco A. Wehrmeister 🆔
Federal University of Technology – Paraná
Curitiba, Paraná, Brazil

Marcelo Götz 🆔
Federal University of Rio Grande do Sul
Porto Alegre, Rio Grande do Sul, Brazil

Achim Rettberg
Hamm-Lippstadt University of Applied
Sciences
Hamm, Germany

ISSN 1868-4238  ISSN 1868-422X  (electronic)
IFIP Advances in Information and Communication Technology
ISBN 978-3-031-34216-5  ISBN 978-3-031-34214-1  (eBook)
https://doi.org/10.1007/978-3-031-34214-1

This Springer imprint is published by the registered company Springer Nature Switzerland AG
The registered company address is: Gewerbestrasse 11, 6330 Cham, Switzerland

# Preface

This book publishes the research and technical works presented at the International Embedded Systems Symposium (IESS) 2022. After a long period of very reduced personal contact due to the worldwide measures to fight the COVID-19 pandemic, we were pleased to hold the seventh edition of IESS as a presential event. We were very happy to once again gather our community together. Deep and fruitful discussions occurred during the event covering several topical aspects of embedded and cyber-physical systems. This book presents tendencies and solutions for problems tightly coupled to industry ranging from new methodologies to novel hardware designs, analysis approaches, engineering artificial intelligence into often-constrained embedded systems, and real-world application examples.

A broad discussion on the design, analysis, and verification of embedded and cyber-physical systems is presented in a complementary view throughout the chapters of this book. The presented research and technical works cover system-level design methods, algorithms, verification and validation techniques, estimation of system properties and characteristics, performance analysis, and real-time systems design. Also, the book presents industrial and real-world application case studies that discuss the challenges and realizations of modern embedded systems, especially when it comes to including artificial intelligence algorithms and techniques in embedded systems.

The technological advances over recent years have provided a resourceful infrastructure to embedded systems in terms of an enormous amount of processing and storage capacity. Formerly external components are now integrated into a single System-on-Chip that includes various hardware accelerators such as video decoders, and artificial intelligence co-processors. This tendency results in a dramatic reduction in the size and cost of embedded systems. Such a hardware infrastructure enables an increasing number of provided services, allowing embedded systems to enter a lot of application areas (including cyber-physical applications). As a unique technology, the design of embedded systems is an essential element of many innovations.

Embedded systems meet their performance goals, including real-time constraints, by employing a combination of special-purpose hardware and software components tailored to the system requirements. Both the development of new features and the reuse of existing intellectual property components are essential to keeping up with ever-increasing customer requirements. Furthermore, design complexity is steadily growing, with an increasing number of components that must cooperate properly. Novel integrated co-design approaches are deemed necessary to further improve the design flow while reducing the project's overall cost.

Embedded system designers must cope with multiple goals and constraints simultaneously, including timing, power, reliability, dependability, maintenance, packaging, and, last but not least, price. Safety, security, and privacy are mandatory requirements for modern applications that also demand different levels of intelligence and autonomy. The significance and importance of these constraints vary depending on the target application area. Typical embedded applications include consumer electronics, automotive, avionics, medical, industrial automation, robotics, communication devices, autonomous transportation systems, and others.

The International Embedded Systems Symposium (IESS) is a unique forum to present novel ideas, exchange timely research results, and discuss the state of the art and future trends in the field of embedded systems. Contributors and participants from both industry and academia take an active part in this symposium. The IESS conference is organized by the Computer Systems Technology committee (TC10) of the International Federation for Information Processing (IFIP), especially the Working Group 10.2 "Embedded Systems".

IESS is a truly interdisciplinary conference on the design of embedded systems. Computer Science and Electrical Engineering are the predominant academic disciplines concerned with the topics covered in IESS, but many applications also involve civil, mechanical, aerospace, and automotive engineering, as well as various medical disciplines.

In 2005, IESS was held for the first time, in Manaus, Brazil. In this initial installment, IESS 2005 was very successful with 30 accepted papers ranging from specification to embedded systems applications. IESS 2007 was the second edition of the symposium, held in Irvine (CA), USA with 35 accepted papers and 2 tutorials ranging from analysis and design methodologies to case studies from automotive and medical applications. IESS 2009 took place in the wonderful Schoß Montfort in Langenargen, Germany with 28 accepted papers and 2 tutorials ranging from efficient modeling to challenges for designers of fault-tolerant embedded systems. IESS 2013 was held in Paderborn, Germany, at the Heinz Nixdorf Museums-Forum (HNF) with 22 full papers and 8 short papers. IESS 2015 was held in Foz do Iguaçu, Brazil, close to the beautiful Iguaçu Falls, with 12 full papers and 6 short papers. In 2019, IESS was held in Friedrichshafen, Germany, with 16 full papers and 4 short papers selected and presented at the symposium.

The seventh edition, IESS 2022, was held in Lippstadt, Germany, in the modern and newly built Innovation Quarter Lippstadt. Currently, this area is attracting a considerable amount of investment for teaching and designing modern and disruptive embedded system applications for the automotive and agricultural sectors. The articles presented in this book are the result of a rigorous review process implemented by the technical program committee. All papers were comprehensively reviewed by three or four experts in the topics covered by each paper. The selection process resulted in 10 full papers and 2 short papers.

The technical program of IESS 2022 included sessions with complementary and interdisciplinary themes, e.g., design methods, model-driven engineering, hardware architectures for embedded systems, and engineering applications of artificial intelligence targeting embedded systems. The technical program included not only remarkably interesting keynotes on actual topics, such as the safe integration of learning in embedded systems, and models for smart cyber-physical systems of systems, but also an invited talk with an industrial focus on how connectivity contributes to smart farming. A very interesting and provocative panel discussion on the future of embedded systems took place and stimulate the attendees to discuss what are the current and future problems regarding embedded systems. Last but not least, the scientific and technical papers were presented and stimulated a deep and insightful discussion between the presenters and the attendees.

First and foremost, we thank our sponsors IFIP WG 10.2 Embedded Systems, Gesellschaft für Informatik e.V. (GI), and Hamm-Lippstadt University of Applied Sciences for their generous financial support of this conference. Without these contributions, IESS 2022 would not have been possible in its current form. We would also like to thank IFIP as the organizational body for the promotion and support of the IESS conference.

Last but not least, we thank the authors for their interesting research contributions and the members of the technical program committee for their valuable time and effort in reviewing the articles. All the editors of this volume cited below, besides their formal roles in the IESS organization, have been involved in the discussions and decisions made about the analysis of review results, the book's organization in sessions, and editing of this preface. Since we are a small group that is involved in the organization of this conference, this has been usual in all previous, as well as for the current IESS edition.

In summary, excited about our strong technical program, we had a highly successful IESS 2022 conference with fruitful and lively discussions.

November 2022

Stefan Henkler<br>
Márcio Kreutz<br>
Marco A. Wehrmeister<br>
Marcelo Götz<br>
Achim Rettberg

# IFIP TC10 Working Conference: International Embedded Systems Symposium (IESS) November 3–4, 2022 Lippstadt, Germany

## General Chairs

Stefan Henkler          University of Applied Sciences Hamm-Lippstadt, Germany
Márcio Kreutz           Federal University of Rio Grande do Norte, Brazil

## Program Chair

Marco A. Wehrmeister    Federal University of Technology Parana, Brazil

## Steering Committee

Michael Amann                   ZF Friedrichshafen, Germany
Jürgen Becker                   University of Karlsruhe, Germany
Christophe Bobda                University of Florida, USA
Luigi Carro                     Federal University of Rio Grande do Sul, Brazil
Florian Dittmann                Stabil Group International GmbH, Germany
Rainer Doemer                   University of California at Irvine, USA
Michel Dos Santos Soares        Federal University of Sergipe, Brazil
Edison P. de Freitas            Federal University of Rio Grande do Sul, Brazil
Masahiro Fujita                 University of Tokyo, Japan
Marcelo Götz                    Federal University of Rio Grande do Sul, Brazil
Andreas Gerstlauer              University of Texas at Austin, USA
Kim Grüttner                    OFFIS, Germany
Stefan Henkler                  University of Applied Science Dortmund, Germany
Paula Herber                    University of Münster, Germany
Carsten Homburg                 dSPACE, Germany
Uwe Honekamp                    Vector Informatik, Germany
Michael Huebner                 Ruhr-University Bochum, Germany
Márcio Kreutz                   Federal University of Rio Grande do Norte, Brazil
Thomas Lehmann                  HAW Hamburg, Germany
Jose Lima                       Polytechnic Institute of Braganca, Portugal
Monica Magalhães Pereira        Federal University of Rio Grande do Norte, Brazil
Marcio Oyamada                  UNIOESTE, Brazil
Carlos E. Pereira               Federal University of Rio Grande do Sul, Brazil
Andy Pimentel                   University of Amsterdam, The Netherlands
Achim Rettberg                  University of Applied Sciences Hamm-Lippstadt, Germany

| Hiroyuki Tomiyama | Ritsumeikan University, Japan |
| Kristian Rother | University of Applied Sciences Hamm-Lippstadt, Germany |
| Antonio Carlos Schneider Beck Filho | Federal University of Rio Grande do Sul, Brazil |
| Wolfgang Schröder-Preikschat | Friedrich-Alexander-Universität Erlangen-Nürnberg, Germany |
| Charles Steinmetz | University of Applied Sciences Hamm-Lippstadt, Germany |
| Flavio Rech Wagner | Federal University of Rio Grande do Sul, Brazil |
| Marco A. Wehrmeister | Federal University of Technology Parana, Brazil |
| Cesar Albenes Zeferino | University of Vale do Itajaí, Brazil |

## Co-organizing Institution

IFIP TC 10, WG 10.2

# Contents

**Design Methods and Model-Driven Engineering**

Evaluating the Perceptual Properties of Crosscutting Concerns Occurrence
Points Specifications in Embedded Software. . . . . . . . . . . . . . . . . . . . . . .    3
   *Marco A. Wehrmeister, Rodrigo S. C. Oliveira, and Douglas B. Renaux*

Simulation of Timing Attacks and Challenges for Early Side-Channel
Security Analysis . . . . . . . . . . . . . . . . . . . . . . . . . . . . . . . . . . . . . . . . .   16
   *Marcel Schoppmeier and Paula Herber*

Adaptation for Energy Saving in Time-Triggered Systems Using
Meta-scheduling with Sample Points . . . . . . . . . . . . . . . . . . . . . . . . . . . .   28
   *Pascal Muoka, Oghenemaro Umuomo, Daniel Onwuchekwa,*
   *and Roman Obermaisser*

Communication Layer Architecture for a Production Line Digital Twin
Using Hierarchical Colored Petri Nets . . . . . . . . . . . . . . . . . . . . . . . . . . .   41
   *Adam Sulak, Charles Steinmetz, and Achim Rettberg*

**Hardware Architectures for Embedded Systems**

Exploiting Heterogeneity in PIM Architectures for Data-Intensive
Applications. . . . . . . . . . . . . . . . . . . . . . . . . . . . . . . . . . . . . . . . . . . . . .   53
   *Rafael Fão de Moura and Luigi Carro*

Demonstrating Scalability of the Checkerboard GPC with SystemC
TLM-2.0 . . . . . . . . . . . . . . . . . . . . . . . . . . . . . . . . . . . . . . . . . . . . . . . . .   65
   *Yutong Wang, Arya Daroui, and Rainer Dömer*

MAFAT: Memory-Aware Fusing and Tiling of Neural Networks
for Accelerated Edge Inference . . . . . . . . . . . . . . . . . . . . . . . . . . . . . . . .   78
   *Jackson Farley and Andreas Gerstlauer*

Memristor-only LSTM Acceleration with Non-linear Activation Functions . . . .   89
   *Rafael Fão de Moura, João Paulo C. de Lima, and Luigi Carro*

Minimizing Memory Contention in an APNG Encoder Using a Grid
of Processing Cells . . . . . . . . . . . . . . . . . . . . . . . . . . . . . . . . . . . . . . . . .  101
   *Vivek Govindasamy, Emad Arasteh, and Rainer Dömer*

## Engineering Applications of Artificial Intelligence Targeting Embedded Systems

Analysing the Characteristics of Neural Networks for the Recognition
of Sugar Beets . . . . . . . . . . . . . . . . . . . . . . . . . . . . . . . . . . . . . . . . . . 115
   *Luca Brodo, Stefan Henkler, and Kristian Rother*

Synthetic Data for Machine Learning on Embedded Systems in Precision
Agriculture. . . . . . . . . . . . . . . . . . . . . . . . . . . . . . . . . . . . . . . . . . . . . . 127
   *Olaniyi Bayonle Alao, Kristian Rother, and Stefan Henkler*

Using Network Architecture Search for Optimizing Tensor Compression . . . . . 139
   *Arunachalam Thirunavukkarasu and Domenik Helms*

**Author Index** . . . . . . . . . . . . . . . . . . . . . . . . . . . . . . . . . . . . . . . . 151

# Design Methods and Model-Driven Engineering

# Evaluating the Perceptual Properties of Crosscutting Concerns Occurrence Points Specifications in Embedded Software

Marco A. Wehrmeister[1,2]([✉]), Rodrigo S. C. Oliveira[1], and Douglas B. Renaux[1]

[1] Universidade Tecnológica Federal do Paraná (UTFPR), Curitiba 80230-901, Brazil
{wehrmeister,douglasrenaux}@utfpr.edu.br, rodrigoo@alunos.utfpr.edu.br
[2] University of Münster, 48149 Münster, Germany
wehrmeister@uni-muenster.de

**Abstract.** Crosscutting concerns associated with the non-functional requirements and system constraints contribute to the growing complexity of embedded software. Techniques, such as *Aspect-Oriented Software Development*, propose units of modularization to encapsulate their handling. A key design issue in embedded software is related to the process of locating, identifying, and specifying the *Crosscutting Concerns Occurrence Points* (CCOP). This paper reports on an empirical evaluation that compares four notations, namely JPDD, Theme/UML, AspectJ, and Tracematch to specify the selection of CCOPs. A set of metrics to quantify the perceptual properties of these specifications was proposed based on the *Physics of Notation* (PoN) conceptual framework. Three embedded automation systems have been specified using the mentioned notations and evaluated according to the proposed metrics set. Experimental results show how the used notation impacts the comprehension of the specification, whether in graphical or textual form. The results show poor discriminability in the cognitive effectiveness of visual representations. Hence, using visual notations to specify CCOP selection seems not to facilitate the understanding as one would expect.

**Keywords:** crosscutting concerns · embedded software · notation for visual and graphical specification · quality model · metrics

## 1 Introduction

In traditional paradigms, including Object-Oriented and Procedural, some of the requirements and system constraints are necessarily scattered across multiple units of modularization In both the design and implementation. This scenario with crosscutting concerns leads to tangled and scattered handling that impact negatively on coupling, cohesion, and the single-responsibility principle. Crosscutting Concerns Occurrence Points (CCOP) indicate the parts of the software where the handling code must be inserted. The various programming languages

S. Henkler et al. (Eds.): IESS 2022, IFIP AICT 669, pp. 3–15, 2023.
https://doi.org/10.1007/978-3-031-34214-1_1

and/or visual notations present diverse linguistic means to identify such CCOP selections. Common ways to specify CCOP selections are based on lexical properties and/or system behavioral or structural context [19, 20].

It is not trivial to understand "when" and "how" the crosscutting concerns are handled and where they occur in the implementation of the system's functional requirements. This is the case of embedded real-time systems that present distinct sorts of crosscutting concerns, non-functional requirements, and constraints [8], such as timing, concurrency, resources monitoring, energy consumption, dependability, and others.

Two approaches are observed in the current state-of-the-art of the specification of system crosscutting concerns: graphical and textual forms. Both forms have been explored particularly in the context of *Aspect-Oriented Software Development* (AOSD) [1,7,10,15]. One technique to identify and specify the selection of CCOPs through a graphical form is the *Join Point Designation Diagrams* (JPDDs) [19], which is based on UML [17]. Similarly, Theme/UML [6] is also based on UML but it supports symmetric separation of concerns rather than asymmetric separation that is supported by most AOSD approaches. Engineers specify *bindings* among *themes* to indicate where the implementation of crosscutting concerns must be inserted in the software execution flow.

However, although UML is widely accepted in the industry, there is no precise semantics when it comes to the specification of crosscutting concerns since UML was created to support the Object-Oriented paradigm, which is known for presenting modularity issues of the crosscutting concerns handling [12]. Consequently, although there are approaches to extend UML semantics towards AOSD [21,22], the result is a quite imprecise specification of the CCOP selections, due to poor discriminability [16], increasing the difficulty in the comprehension and maintenance of the artifacts generated.

This paper reports an empirical evaluation that compares four AOSD notations, namely JPDD, Theme/UML, AspectJ, and Tracematch, when specifying implicitly or explicitly the CCOP selections. The goal is to assess how the mentioned techniques facilitate the comprehension of the CCOP selection specification, whether in graphical or textual form. A quality model, based on the *"Physics of Notation"* (PoN) conceptual framework [16], was proposed; it includes nine metrics that quantify the specification of fifteen CCOP commonly found in embedded software. These CCOPs are related to timing, distributed processing, performance, resource usage monitoring, and control [8,13].

The remainder of this paper is organized as follows. Section 2 overviews briefly the PoN conceptual framework. Section 3 examines previous work and compares their characteristics. Section 4 presents the proposed quality model and its framework to evaluate the specification of CCOP selection. Section 5 presents the empirical evaluation and analyses its results, whereas Sect. 6 discusses the possible threats to the validity of this evaluation. Finally, Sect. 7 draws conclusions and provides an outlook on future works.

## 2   Overview of the Physics of Notations Framework

The conceptual framework *Physics of Notations* (PoN) [16] aims to provide a scientific basis for a design rationale of visual notations in software engineering. To overcome what PoN's authors identified as issues of visual representations being historically ignored and undervalued as well as the lack of discussion on visual syntax, PoN addresses the physical and perceptual properties of notations rather than their logical properties. Therefore, PoN comprises nine design principles that can be summarized as follows:

- **Semiotic Clarity:** there should be a 1:1 correspondence between semantic constructs and graphical symbols;
- **Perceptual Discriminability:** different symbols should be clearly distinguishable from each other;
- **Semantic Transparency:** the appearance of visual representations must suggest their meaning;
- **Complexity Management:** the number of visual elements must be restricted to avoid cognitive overload;
- **Cognitive Integration:** the language must provide mechanisms to explicitly integrate information from multiple diagrams;
- **Visual Expressiveness:** the use of the full range and capacities of visual variables;
- **Dual coding:** a notation should combine text and graphics to improve information conveyance and its understanding;
- **Graphic Economy:** the number of different graphical symbols should be cognitively manageable;
- **Cognitive Fit:** a notation should provide different means to represent the information to better suit different tasks and audiences.

## 3   Related Work

Dealing with crosscutting concerns due to non-functional requirements is a challenge that is still being addressed [20]. Embedded systems present an increasing number of crosscutting concerns that impact several characteristics of the embedded software artifacts and also of the system as a whole [5,13,21]. The Providentia [5] deals with the non-functional requirements and their crosscutting concerns in the design of self-adapting systems that experience various sources of uncertainty. Hannousse [9] proposes a component-based software engineering approach to support explicitly the crosscutting and dynamic features. These are identified early in the process and modeled separately using AOSD concepts to improve components' reusability and maintainability.

   The work in [18] addresses the safety crosscutting concerns within the design process of distributed vehicular control systems, aiming for fault-tolerant and fault-diagnostic mechanisms to improve reliability in communication protocols. The RT-FRIDA framework allows for modeling faults in early-design phases such as requirements engineering. The results show improved fault modeling by handling the associated crosscutting concerns. Similarly, Zahng et al. [24] propose a knowledge-driven method for requirements elicitation in cyber-physical systems design. The aim is to identify the implicit non-functional requirements and crosscutting concerns, which are later modeled using SysML requirement diagram. Additionlly, in [3], security and safety crosscutting concerns of safety-critical embedded systems are addressed using design patterns and templates. COOP are specified within the design pattern. Once the design patterns are applied, the crosscutting concern handling elements are intermixed with the system's functional requirements implementation.

Furthermore, there are several distinct proposed approaches to specify CCOP selection, particularly in the context of AOSD. *AspectJ* [12] is a textual programming language that extends Java to define a dynamic crosscutting mechanism in the execution of a program.

*Join Point Designation Diagram* [19] is a modeling approach to visualize join point selections based on the UML semantics. Diagrams of the system events, object symbols, and object flow edges through the adoption of action symbols represent the flow to reach a CCOP. Although JPDD allows specifying CCOP selections uniformly and independently from the programming language, the visual notation is slightly different from the standard, requiring learning effort.

*Theme/UML* [4,6] is a UML-based approach that supports symmetric separation of concerns. A concern is represented as fragments of behavior and structure encapsulated into a single theme. The themes are bound to each other to indicate which elements are affected by elements of other themes. Such bindings are specified manually by the designers. This approach is similar to a join point specification and the relation between functional elements that are affected by aspects. However, it lacks scalability and hinders model comprehension, maintainability, and evolution in large systems.

*Tracematch* [2] is a textual approach that implements regular expressions over the program's execution traces based on a symbols alphabet. Once the regular expression matches an execution trace, an event triggers the execution of a modular unit of crosscutting implementation. Tracematch is a seamless extension to AspectJ. However, although Tracematch innovates in its treatment of free variables in trace patterns, its usage is nontrivial.

Literature review on crosscutting concerns [14] gathers existing quality measures that validate the effectiveness of different techniques. The authors conclude that there is a critical lack of standard benchmarks for the specification of join point selections, hindering the empirical evaluation of the methods and the objective comparison and validation of the research. On the other hand, [25] proposes a quantitative method to evaluate the non-functional requirements and associated crosscutting concerns. The authors report that their approach shortens the time for non-functional requirements evaluation.

A major issue in the understanding of a CCOP selection specification is the lack of knowledge on the underlying paradigm used to encapsulate the crosscutting concerns handling, e.g., Aspect Oriented Paradigm (AOP) [11] from which the concept of join points was derived. The relationship between modeling level

Table 1. Comparison of AOSD techniques. "X" means supported

| | Structural CCOP | | Behavioral CCOP | | Simple Pointcut | | Composite Pointcut | | Quantification Method | | | Position Indication | | | Abstraction | |
|---|---|---|---|---|---|---|---|---|---|---|---|---|---|---|---|---|
| | Static | Dynamic | Static | Dynamic | Graphical | Textual | Graphical | Textual | Declarative | Imperative | Enumeration | Before | Around | After | High | Low |
| AspectJ | | X | | X | | X | | X | X | | | X | X | X | X | X |
| JPDD | X | | X | X | X | | X | | | | | X | X | X | X | |
| Theme/UML | X | | X | X | | | | | X | | X | | | | X | |
| TraceMatch | | X | | X | | X | X | X | X | | | X | X | X | X | X |

and execution level is less clear than in the case of programming languages. Table 1 compares AspectJ, JPDD, Theme/UML, and Tracematch according to the characteristics presented in the existing AOSD literature [20, 23].

To the best of our knowledge, this research is the first that evaluates distinct graphical and textual notations for CCOP selection specification in the light of the PoN conceptual framework. No other empirical studies analyze the perceptual properties of notations related to CCOP (e.g., join points) using quantitative metrics. This is particularly relevant in embedded software since embedded systems do present an intrinsic number of non-functional requirements that lead to concerns that crosscut the system behavior and provided services [8].

## 4　Evaluation Framework

The software engineering literature provides several metrics and evaluation frameworks to extract quantitative information from software artifacts. However, to the best of our knowledge, there is no evaluation framework or quality model created from the perspective of the PoN framework. Therefore, we propose the *Metrics Suite for PoN conceptual framework* (MS4PoN). Its goal is to quantify the perceptual properties of graphical and textual notations to specify CCOP selections and to assess the cognitive effectiveness of specifications. Figure 1 presents the proposed quality model; five principles of the PoN framework are associated with nine metrics. The MS4PoN measures features of graphical and textual notations for specifying CCOP selections in terms of elements, symbols, and syntax:

- **Number of elements (NE):** this metric counts the number of elements contained in the CCOP selection model or the implementation regardless of the specification is in a textual or graphical form. The greater is the NE, the more complex the model or implementation will be.
- **Number of Logical Expressions (NLE):** this metric is defined as the number of agnostic (or abstract) logical expressions specified in the CCOP selection model or implementation. Logical expressions indicate selection criteria. In the experiments, the NLE values are equal for each CCOP despite

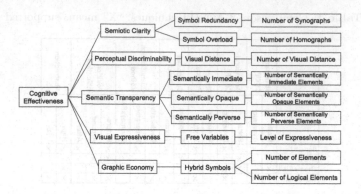

**Fig. 1.** Cognitive effectiveness quality model

the notation used. The objective here is to have an abstract expression representing the selection criterion that shall be specified in the model or the implementation. NLE allows for generating some ratios to be analyzed to provide more precise and homogeneous results.

- **Number of Visual Distance (NVD):** this metric quantifies the number of different syntactic elements specified in the CCOP selection model. In general, the greater the number of the different elements specified in the model or implementation the greater is the NVD, and consequently the faster and more accurately the specification is recognized and understood.

- **Number of Semantically Immediate Elements (NSIE):** this metric determines the total number of semantically immediate elements specified in the CCOP selection model or implementation. An element is semantically immediate if it is easy to infer its meaning from its appearance or mnemonic. The greater the NSIE, the easier it is to understand the model or implementation. A semantically immediate element or symbol must have in its nature an association with: (i) *functional similarities*, e.g., the element method "before()" in AspectJ means to do something before; or (ii) *metaphors*, e.g., a stick figure may represent a person in the UML's use case diagrams; or (iii) any *cultural associations*, e.g., a big "X" in the UML's sequence diagram means a closed communication.

- **Number of Semantically Opaque Elements (NSOE):** the number of semantically opaque elements specified in the CCOP selection model or implementation. An element is semantically opaque or conventional if there is a purely arbitrary relationship between its appearance and its meaning. The greater is the NSOE, the more neutral or conventional elements are being used in the model or implementation, e.g., the excessive use of rectangles in Theme/UML diagrams. This metric represents the zero point in the scale between NSIE and NSPE. It does not augment the perception, but also does not suggest a different meaning from its appearance, and hence, it is a conventional element that must be learned.

- **Number of Semantically Perverse Elements (NSPE):** this metric quantifies the number of semantically perverse elements specified in the CCOP selection model or implementation. An element is semantically perverse or false mnemonic if the opposite meaning is inferred from its appearance. The greater the NSPE, the worst it is to understand the model or implementation. A semantically perverse element or symbol has in its nature lexical properties or false mnemonics that can suggest to a novice reader to infer a different meaning from its appearance. Some UML conventions present this undesirable property, e.g., the UML's package merge.
- **Level of Expressiveness (LVE):** this metric determines the number of visual variables used in a notation for the CCOP selection model or implementation. The LVE counts the number of communication variables used in visual languages, e.g., shape, texture, color, etc. According to [16], LVE values range from zero to eight. Hence, the greater the LVE, the more efficient the model is using the advantage of its being graphical. Conversely, the lower the LVE, the closer the graphical notation is from of the textual one.
- **Number of Synographs (NS):** this metric is defined as the total number of synographs specified in the CCOP selection model or implementation. A synograph element occurs when there is a redundancy in the use of symbols or elements to represent the same semantic construct, e.g., interfaces in UML diagrams. The greater the NS, the more difficult it is to understand the model or implementation. A notation satisfies the requirements of a notational system if it provides a one-to-one correspondence between symbols and their associated concepts [16]. The synograph element is an anomaly that occurs when there is not such one-to-one correspondence thus leading to redundancy of symbols and reduces the understanding of the specification.
- **Number of Homographs (NH):** determines the total number of homographs specified in the CCOP selection model. A homograph occurs when there is an overload in the semantic constructs that can be represented by the same symbols or elements. The greater the NH, the more difficult it is to understand the model. This is the worst type of anomaly as it leads to ambiguity and the potential for misinterpretation [16]. Theme/UML presents such anomaly as the same graphical convention (e.g., rectangle) is used to represent several distinct elements in the specification of CCOP selections: subject, class, behavior symbol in life lines, and aspectual representations.

These metrics are combined to allow evaluating the five principles defined in the PoN framework. *Semiotic Clarity* principle is defined by *Symbol Redundancy* and *Symbol Overload*. The former is impacted by the number of synographs (NS) (visual equivalent of synonyms) found in the specification of CCOP selections, while the latter by the number of homographs (NH) (visual equivalent of homonyms). *Perceptual Discriminability* principle is defined by *Visual Distance* which is directly affected by the Number of Visual Distance (NVD) elements. *Semiotic Transparency* principle is influenced by the number of elements considered *Semantically Immediate* (NSIE), or *Semantically Opaque* (NSOE), and *Semantically Perverse* (NSPE). Ideally, a notation should present the greatest possible number of semantically immediate elements and zero semantically perverse elements. The *Visual Expressiveness* principle is influenced by *Free Variables*, which are directly affected by the number of visual communication channels (Level of Expressiveness - LVE) used to specify CCOP selections. A notation with no visual variables is called *non-visual* (or textual), whereas a notation that uses all visual variables is considered *visually saturated*. The *Graphic Economy* principle is defined by *Hybrid Symbols*, which are directly affected by the number of elements (NE) and number of logical expressions (NLE). A notation with a great number of elements increases its complexity according to how many elements are used per logical expression.

The other PoN principles are not relevant to this work's goals and scope since it addresses the evaluation of CCOP selection specification. *Complexity management* principle cannot be applicable here because we analyze only the part of the notation that deals with CCOP selection; not the whole language. *Cognitive integration* is not relevant to our evaluation because it refers to languages that use multiple diagrams to specify the system requirements. This is not the case for CCOP selection specification since it is often described in a single artifact/document. Finally, regarding *cognitive fit* and *dual coding* principles, we understand that such characteristics are uncountable, i.e., either a given notation presents these characteristics or not.

## 5   Empirical Experiments and Results

MS4PoN has been employed to evaluate two graphical (JPDD and Theme/UML) and two textual (AspectJ and Tracematch) notations to specify CCOP selection. The goal is to evaluate the cognitive effectiveness and the perceptual properties of these notations by employing the quality model and calculating the MS4PoN metrics described in the previous section.

The data source for these experiments includes fifteen CCOP commonly found in the software for embedded real-time cyber-physical systems [8,13,21, 22]. In summary, these CCOP appear in various pieces of the embedded software: (a) the structure definition, the instantiation, and the behavior of active objects; (b) the structure definition, and the exclusive access to passive objects' data and services; (c) read/write access to objects' attributes; and (d) subsystems initialization. These CCOP have been (re)used in three case studies: (i) the movement control system of an unmanned aerial vehicle; (ii) the control system of an industrial packing system; and, (iii) the movement control system of an automated wheelchair. The experiments consist of creating four specifications (JPDD, Theme/UML, AspectJ, and Tracematch) for each CCOP. A total of 60 distinct specifications have been created. MS4PoN metrics have been calculated for each distinct specification. Although these notations allow for a complete AOSD specification, the experiments and its results consider only the parts of the notations related to the specification of CCOP selections. Experimental data and results are available in https://tinyurl.com/v4b5y42s.

**Table 2.** Metrics for 60 specifications of CCOP selection

| Notation | NE | NLE | NVD | NSIE | NSOE | NSPE | LVE | NS | NH |
|----------|-----|-----|-----|------|------|------|------|----|-----|
| AspectJ | 201 | 72 | 201 | 28 | 201 | 0 | 0.00 | 0 | 0 |
| JPDD | 87 | 72 | 55 | 0 | 55 | 22 | 1.33 | 0 | 16 |
| Theme/UML | 360 | 72 | 45 | 0 | 90 | 15 | 2.00 | 15 | 150 |
| Tracematch | 141 | 73 | 141 | 53 | 141 | 0 | 0.00 | 0 | 3 |

**Table 3.** Ratio between MS4PoN metrics. Bold text indicates the better values.

| Ratios | AspectJ | JPDD | Theme/UML | Tracematch |
|--------|---------|------|-----------|------------|
| NE/NLE | 2.792 | **1.208** | 5.000 | 1.932 |
| NVD/NE | **1.000** | 0.632 | 0.125 | **1.000** |
| NVD/NLE | 2.792 | 0.764 | 0.625 | **1.932** |
| NSIE/NE | 0.139 | 0.000 | 0.000 | **0.376** |
| NSIE/NLE | 0.389 | 0.000 | 0.000 | **0.726** |
| NSOE/NE | **1.000** | 0.632 | 0.250 | **1.000** |
| NSOE/NLE | **2.792** | 0.764 | 1.250 | **1.932** |
| NSPE/NE | **0.000** | 0.253 | 0.042 | **0.000** |
| NSPE/NLE | **0.000** | 0.306 | 0.208 | **0.000** |
| LVE | 0.000 | 1.333 | **2.000** | 0.000 |
| NS/NE | **0.000** | **0.000** | 0.042 | **0.000** |
| NS/NLE | **0.000** | **0.000** | 0.208 | **0.000** |
| NH/NE | **0.000** | 0.184 | 0.417 | 0.021 |
| NH/NLE | **0.000** | 0.222 | 2.083 | 0.041 |

Table 2 shows MS4PoN metrics calculated on the 60 specifications of the considered COOP. These values represent the sum of individual values of each metric for each specification of CCOP selection. The exception is LVE value which is calculated as an average value. LVE represents the visual expressiveness of the notation according to PoN framework [16], whose value should range from zero to eight. Summing LVE of the distinct specifications does not represent properly the visual expressiveness concept because it would indicate often a saturated notation (i.e. a value greater than 8) as the number of considered specifications increases.

To better analyze and compare the results, we created some ratios between metrics to quantify the cognitive effectiveness of a notation under the PoN perspective. Such ratios (see Table 3) intend to identify how the perceptual properties are distributed over the elements described within the specifications.

NVD/NE ratio indicates how many different syntactic elements appear per element in the notation. The textual notations (AspectJ and Tracematch) have a higher value than visual notations (JPDD and Theme/UML). This means that

AspectJ and Tracematch employ more different syntactic elements per element. The same reasoning is valid for the NVD/NLE ratio that considers the number of different syntactic elements per logical expression. The higher the visual distance per logical expression is, the better it is to understand the specification. However, it is important to highlight that a good value for these ratios should be close to one, i.e., the notation has only one distinct element per logical expression. Values between zero and one mean that there are implicit elements within the specification, and values greater than one mean that the notation is verbose. Both situations somehow hinder the understanding of the specification.

NSIE-related ratios indicate how many semantically immediate elements are used per element or per logical expression in the specification. These ratios identify how easily one can infer the correct meaning of the elements described in the specification by their appearance. For instance, the NSIE/NE ratio for Tracematch and AspectJ are a bit higher than the others, i.e., they have more elements (in the specification) that present an implicit understanding of their semantics compared to JPDD and Theme/UML. On the other hand, NSPE-related ratio indicate a higher number of perverse elements in JPDD and Theme/UML. This might be due to the fact that JPDD and Theme/UML are extensions of UML. According to [16], the majority of UML notations were not designed considering the perceptual and cognitive properties that graphical notation must have.

By analyzing the ratios presented in Table 2, Tracematch and AspectJ seem to be more effective regarding the understanding and comprehension than JPDD and Theme/UML to specify CCOP selections. These empirical quantitative results might indicate that the specification of CCOP selections through a graphical notation has poor discriminability on the cognitive effectiveness of visual representations. Under the PoN framework perspective, it seems that using graphical notations makes the COOP selection specification difficult to understand, especially when the engineers are not skilled enough on the visual notation.

# 6    Limitations and Threats to Validity

Although the obtained results provide adequate support for this work's conclusions, some factors may have influenced the conducted evaluation, as is usual in any empirical study. Threats to the internal validity of the evaluation may arise from the fact that the cognitive effectiveness results may be influenced by the authors' experience. Such an issue presents a low risk to affect negatively the results obtained since (a) the proposed quality model and the experimental results are based on the perspective of the consolidated PoN framework rather than on the authors' own experience, and (b) the CCOP used in the experiment are from real-world case studies carried out in previous works. However, it is worth mentioning that NSIE, NSPE, and NSOP would be seen as subjective metrics. Thus, they may be influenced by the authors' experience. Although there may be differences if other engineers evaluate the same specifications, these metrics values might not differ substantially from those presented here since the metrics evaluate the notations' syntax rather than semantics The values of these metrics are also reasonable fair with respect to the notation features they measure, but they must be analyzed carefully. As they are 3 out of 9 MS4PoN metrics, the authors understand that the obtained results are valid regarding the assessment of cognitive effectiveness of the evaluated notations to specify COOP selection.

Another threat to validity may concern the generality of the results. The proposed quality model and MS4PoN metrics might be of general application. Thus, they may be used to assess other visual and textual notations. Although the results discussed here are limited to the three studies cases from the embedded software domain, the variety of CCOP types used in the experiments allows us to believe that similar results may be obtained in other application domains when it comes to specifying CCOP selection. The authors consider to be low the probability of this risk influencing this work's findings as the experiments' scope was limited to embedded software systems. Although the planned experiments have been carefully conducted to achieve this work's goals, other studies and experiments involving other notations and contexts are still necessary.

## 7    Conclusions and Future Work

This work evaluates the perceptual properties of graphical and textual notations of different techniques (AspectJ, JPDD, Theme/UML, and Tracematch) towards the CCOP selection specification. For that, a quality model and a metrics suit (MS4PoN) have been proposed based on the PoN conceptual framework [16].

Experimental results showed empirical evidence that the graphical specification of CCOP selections has poor discriminability on the cognitive effectiveness of visual representations. The graphical notations evaluated in the experiments present a great number of homographs elements to specify CCOP selections. The homographs are anomalies that lead to ambiguity and misinterpretations [16].

The visual distance of the evaluated graphical notation falls short of what was expected. Results show a maximum of 0.764 different graphic elements per logical expression. This means that most of the visual elements are equal or similar, affecting the understanding and cognition of the engineers. On the other hand, one of the evaluated textual notations (AspectJ) shows an interesting ratio of 2.792, meaning that for each logical expression there are 2.792 textual syntactic elements that are different among themselves. In addition, Tracematch (textual notation) presented the highest NSIE among the techniques compared in this work. This is quite impressive as the textual notations present more immediate elements (i.e., syntactical elements associated to a mnemonic) than visual notations. It means that textual notations are more comprehensive than visual notations for specifying CCOP selections in spite of Tracematch presented a low NH that impacts negatively the cognition but, in comparison with the visual notations, the difference is not meaningful.

Another result that drew our attention is the many semantically perverse elements (NSPE) of the evaluated graphical notations. In JPDD, and particularly in Theme/UML, the specification of CCOP selections includes elements or symbols whose correct semantic has a false mnemonic. Thus, a novice engineer may infer a different meaning from its appearance. The level of expressiveness (LVE) of the evaluated graphical notations is very low, close to a textual notation, since they present few variables of visual communication (e.g., shape, color, texture, etc.). This is below the expectations since JPDD and Theme/UML seem not to benefit from the expected advantages of a visual language. According to [16], this is similar to the majority of the visual notations in software engineering.

As future work, we plan to evaluate other graphical and textual notations, not only for specifying more complex CCOP selections but also other features. It is also important is to perform experiments with novice and experienced designers to further assess the proposed quality model and MS4PON metrics. Also, given that the graphical notations seem to fail to improve the understanding of CCOP selection, we are developing a new technique to specify CCOP selections with a mix of textual and graphical elements (i.e. dual coding [16]), aiming to increase the cognitive effectiveness of its perceptual properties.

# References

1. Acreţoaie, V., Störrle, H., Strüber, D.: VMTL: a language for end-user model transformation. Softw. Syst. Model. **17**(4), 1139–1167 (2018)
2. Allan, C., et al.: Adding trace matching with free variables to AspectJ. In: Proceedings of SIGPLAN Conference on Object-Oriented Programming, Systems, Languages, and Applications, pp. 345–364. ACM, New York (2005)
3. Armoush, A.: Towards the integration of security and safety patterns in the design of safety-critical embedded systems. In: 2022 4th International Conference on Applied Automation and Industrial Diagnostics (ICAAID), vol. 1, pp. 1–6 (2022)
4. Baniassad, E., Clarke, S.: Theme: an approach for aspect-oriented analysis and design. In: 26th International Conference on Software Engineering, pp. 158–167. IEEE (2004)
5. Bowers, K.M., et al.: Providentia: using search-based heuristics to optimize satisficement and competing concerns between functional and non-functional objectives in self-adaptive systems. J. Syst. Softw. **162**, 110497 (2020)
6. Clarke, S.: Extending standard UML with model composition semantics. Sci. Comput. Program. **44**(1), 71–100 (2002)
7. Filman, R., Elrad, T., Clarke, S., Akşit, M. (eds.): Aspect-Oriented Software Development, 1st edn. Addison-Wesley Professional (2004)
8. de Freitas, E.P., Wehrmeister, M.A., Silva, E.T., Carvalho, F.C., Pereira, C.E., Wagner, F.R.: DERAF: a high-level aspects framework for distributed embedded real-time systems design. In: Moreira, A., Grundy, J. (eds.) EAW 2007. LNCS, vol. 4765, pp. 55–74. Springer, Heidelberg (2007). https://doi.org/10.1007/978-3-540-76811-1_4
9. Hannousse, A.: A development process for component software with crosscutting and dynamic features. In: 2019 International Conference on Theoretical and Applicative Aspects of Computer Science (ICTAACS), vol. 1, pp. 1–8, December 2019
10. Khan, M.U., Sartaj, H., Iqbal, M.Z., Usman, M., Arshad, N.: AspectOCL: using aspects to ease maintenance of evolving constraint specification. Empir. Softw. Eng. **24**(4), 2674–2724 (2019)

11. Kiczales, G., et al.: Aspect-oriented programming. In: Proceedings of European Conference on Object-Oriented Programming (ECOOP). LNCS 1241. Springer (1997)
12. Kiczales, G., Hilsdale, E., Hugunin, J., Kersten, M., Palm, J., Griswold, W.G.: An overview of AspectJ. In: Knudsen, J.L. (ed.) ECOOP 2001. LNCS, vol. 2072, pp. 327–354. Springer, Heidelberg (2001). https://doi.org/10.1007/3-540-45337-7_18
13. Leite, M., Wehrmeister, M.A.: System-level design based on UML/MARTE for FPGA-based embedded real-time systems. Des. Autom. Embed. Syst. 20(2), 127–153 (2016). https://doi.org/10.1007/s10617-016-9172-6
14. McFadden, R.R., Mitropoulos, F.J.: Survey of aspect mining case study software and benchmarks. In: 2013 Proceedings of IEEE SoutheastCon, pp. 1–5, April 2013
15. Mongiovì, M., Pappalardo, G., Tramontana, E.: Specifying and identifying widely used crosscutting concerns. Knowl.-Based Syst. 126, 20–32 (2017)
16. Moody, D.: The "physics" of notations: toward a scientific basis for constructing visual notations in software engineering 35(6), 756–779 (2009)
17. Object Management Group (OMG): Unified Modeling Language version 2.5.1 (2017). https://www.omg.org/spec/UML/2.5.1/
18. dos Santos Roque, A., et al.: An approach to address safety as non-functional requirements in distributed vehicular control systems. J. Control Autom. Electric. Syst. 30(5), 700–715 (2019)
19. Stein, D., Hanenberg, S., Unland, R.: Join point designation diagrams: a graphical representation of join point selections. Int. J. Software Eng. Knowl. Eng. 16(03), 317–346 (2006)
20. Tariq, S., et al.: Approaches for non-functional requirement modeling: a literature survey. In: International Conference on Computing & Information Sciences, pp. 1–6 (2021)
21. Wehrmeister, M.A., Pereira, C.E., Rammig, F.J.: Aspect-oriented model-driven engineering for embedded systems applied to automation systems. IEEE Trans. Industr. Inf. 9(4), 2373–2386 (2013). https://doi.org/10.1109/TII.2013.2240308
22. Wehrmeister, M.A., et al.: Combining aspects and object-orientation in model-driven engineering for distributed industrial mechatronics systems. Mechatronics 24(7), 844–865 (2014). https://doi.org/10.1016/j.mechatronics.2013.12.008
23. Wimmer, M., et al.: A survey on UML-based aspect-oriented design modeling. ACM Comput. Surv. 43(4), 28:1–28:33 (2011)
24. Zhang, Y., et al.: Non-functional requirements elicitation based on domain knowledge graph for automatic code generation of industrial cyber-physical systems. In: 47th Conference of the IEEE Industrial Electronics Society, pp. 1–6 (2021)
25. Zhou, Z., et al.: An evaluation of quantitative non-functional requirements assurance using ArchiMate. IEEE Access 8, 72395–72410 (2020)

# Simulation of Timing Attacks and Challenges for Early Side-Channel Security Analysis

Marcel Schoppmeier and Paula Herber[✉]

University of Münster, Einsteinstr. 62, 48149 Münster, Germany
{marcel.schoppmeier,paula.herber}@uni-muenster.de

**Abstract.** Side-channel attacks (SCA) enable attackers to gain access to non-disclosed information by measuring emissions of a system, e.g., timing, electromagnetic waves or power consumption. The emissions of a system can typically only be measured on the final system. As a consequence, the analysis of such security threats is often only possible at a very late stage in the development process. In this paper, we present an approach to simulate timing attacks in early stages of the development process with SystemC and discuss the potentials and limitations of this approach. Our results show that the simulation of SCA in SystemC is generally possible, but currently difficult due to an explanation gap. It is, to the best of our knowledge, not well understood where the causal connection between physical quantities and data, which is exploited in SCA, comes from. This poses a major challenge for the design of precise models that accurately reflect physical insights for early security analysis.

**Keywords:** Side-Channel Attacks · Modeling and Simulation · SystemC

## 1 Introduction

Many cyber-physical systems (CPS) are safety-critical (e.g. cars or airplanes) or handle sensitive data (e.g. cryptowallets or health monitoring devices). Thus, it is important that they are secured against malicious attacks. In side-channel attacks (SCA), the attacker extracts non-disclosed information provided by emissions of the CPS, e.g., timing information, power consumption, electromagnetic waves, sound or other output signals. Securing CPS against SCA is difficult for two major reasons: First, CPS are directly exposed to the attacker and offer a large attack surface. Second, how strongly secret information correlates with hardware activities can not easily be analyzed early in the development process because the emissions of a system can only be measured for the produced system. Second, a prerequisite to model and simulate CPS and analyze vulnerabilities early is a detailed model of their attack surface and the physical information that might be exploited with SCA. Such a model usually does not exist.

In this paper, we present a modeling and simulation approach for timing attacks using the system level design language SystemC. Our key idea is to

© IFIP International Federation for Information Processing 2023
Published by Springer Nature Switzerland AG 2023
S. Henkler et al. (Eds.): IESS 2022, IFIP AICT 669, pp. 16–27, 2023.
https://doi.org/10.1007/978-3-031-34214-1_2

describe the system and its physical emissions on a comparatively high level of abstraction. In this way, we can identify side-channel vulnerabilities early in the design process. SystemC [8] is a C++ library and provides an event-driven simulation interface. This enables the simulation of an hardware-software-co-design on various levels of abstraction. We chose SystemC as a library for the simulation of physical quantities because it offers the possibility to simulate CPS in an early design phase. Results can be achieved with suitable models of physical quantities, which serve to assess the security. Furthermore, modeling can be specified and implemented on a more concrete design level if the required information is available. However, as physical information is only abstractly available in early design stages, an attack or related physical information that is not precisely captured cannot provide any insights into system security. In order to investigate this in more detail, we added physical information in several steps to be able to examine what effect it has on the capabilites to model an attack. This enabled us to identify details that are important when modeling physical attacks. We have visualized the results such that we could compare and analyze them. As a representative exemplary attack, we chose the timing attack by Kocher [10], which is the first and most cited publication on this topic.

The rest of this paper is structured as follows: In Sect. 2, we introduce preliminaries. In Sect. 3, we discuss related work. In Sect. 4, we present our approach for modeling and simulation of timing attacks in SystemC. Then, we discuss modeling and simulation of other SCA. We conclude in Sect. 5.

## 2   Overview: Side-Channel and Timing Attacks

A SCA is a security exploit that gathers information from side-channels, e.g., from cache data or from physical parameters like power consumption, execution time, electromagnetic emission, noise or light [16]. This information is used to deduce secrets of a CPS (for example, a keyphrase) by analyzing the observed data. This is possible because there is often a correlation between the measured data and the hidden internal state of the processing device, which is itself related to the secret key. As an attack is very specific to a given implementation, SCA are less general, but often much more powerful than classical cryptanalysis. A secure system depends not only on an encryption algorithm, but also on its implementation and the hardware that is used during execution, which should not allow conclusions about processed data. To perform traditional SCA, the attacker usually needs physical access to the device. In recent years, remote software execution via apps or websites is attacked more frequently. Modern SCA target potentially millions of devices at the same time [16].

A commonly used taxonomy of SCA [1] distinguishes between invasive (e.g. reverse engineering) and non-invasive (e.g. fault injection, traffic analysis) attacks, and between passive (e.g. timing, traffic, power analysis) and active (e.g. fault injection) attacks. In this paper, we focus on non-invasive passive attacks.

```
1    // Compute y = x^d (mod N) where d = d_0d_1d_2...d_n in binary, with d_0 = 1
2    s = x
3    for i = 1 to n
4        s = s^2 (mod N)
5        if d_i == 1 then
6            s = s · x (mod N)
7        end if
8    next i
9    return(s)
```

**Fig. 1.** The square-and-multiply algorithm [17]

## Timing Attacks

During a timing attack, the execution time of a system for varying inputs is used to deduce non-disclosed information. The execution time differs for varying inputs because an implemented algorithm often performs computations in non-constant time. Logical operations, e.g. used for memory accesses, arithmetic operations, comparisons or conditional statements consume varying time. Another reason are performance optimizations by the compiler. The resulting timing variations can leak information about the observed system. For example, with some knowledge about the implementation, statistical analysis can reveal private keys of cryptosystems in an inexpensive way. Timing attacks have a special position among SCA because they can be applied remotely, through a network.

A representative example of a timing attack is Kocher's approach to attack Diffie-Hellman and RSA private key operations that use the square-and-multiply algorithm [10], which is shown in Fig. 1. In the timing attack presented by Kocher, the attacker makes use of the fact that the algorithm performs the multiplication and modulo operation in Line 6 only if the bit position of the private key contains a one.

To model such an attack early in the development process requires a precise model of the underlying physical effects. In the following, we describe the exact procedure of the attack based on Sects. 2, 4 and 5 of [10]. However, we have slightly refined the explanation of how it is possible to identify correctly guessed exponent bits, since in [10] this topic is only dealt with superficially.

In the first step, we start to attack $d_1$ which is the first unknown bit we want to find out. First, for a given $j$ and messages $y_0, \ldots, y_j$, we measure how much time the algorithm takes for each individual message so that we get the corresponding timing measurements $T_0, \ldots, T_j$. Second, we simulate the time it takes to execute all known bits and the following unknown exponent bit. Thereby, we obtain two different simulation times $TS0$ and $TS1$ for each message, since there are two options for the last simulated bit. Third, we calculate the variance of the difference between the timing measurements and the simulation times:

$$\mathrm{Var}\,[T - TS0] := \frac{1}{n} \sum_{i=0}^{j} ((T_i - TS0_i) - \mathrm{E}\,[T - TS0])^2$$

$$\mathrm{Var}\,[T - TS1] := \frac{1}{n} \sum_{i=0}^{j} ((T_i - TS1_i) - \mathrm{E}\,[T - TS1])^2$$

(1)

The crucial observation in [10] is that a correctly-emulated iteration reduces the expected variance, since iterations followed by a false exponent bit increases the variance. This identifies the correct exponent bit.

We want to elucidate this issue in more detail and in more general terms by not only estimating a bit, but an arbitrary number. Let therefore $w$ be the number of total bits of the private key, $b$ the number of guessed bits and $c$ the number of the first exponent bit guesses that are still correct. Then, the difference between the timing measurement and the simulation time of one message can be described as follows. Hereby, $t_j$ is the time required for one algorithm iteration for bit $j$, $a_j$ is the time for a wrong guess for bit $j$. We do not consider timing errors like measurement errors or loop overhead for simplification.

If b was guessed correctly, the following applies:

$$T_i - TS_i = \sum_{j=0}^{w-1} t_j - \sum_{j=0}^{b-1} t_j = \sum_{j=b}^{w-1} t_j$$

If otherwise only guesses right up to exponent bit position $c - 1$ are correct, the difference is composed as follows:

$$T_i - TS_i = \sum_{j=0}^{w-1} t_j - \sum_{j=0}^{c-1} t_j - \sum_{j=c}^{b-1} a_j$$

$$= \sum_{j=0}^{w-1} t_j - \sum_{j=0}^{c-1} t_j - \underbrace{\sum_{j=c}^{b-1} t_j + \sum_{j=c}^{b-1} t_j}_{0} - \sum_{j=c}^{b-1} a_j$$

$$= \sum_{j=b}^{w-1} t_j + \sum_{j=c}^{b-1} t_j - \sum_{j=c}^{b-1} a_j$$

$$= \sum_{j=b}^{w-1} t_j + \sum_{j=c}^{b-1} (t_j - a_j)$$

If we now consider both results, we can understand why the variance should be higher in the second case. The incorrectly guessed bits can both lead to the second summand being positive or negative, which leads to higher deviations.

In his experimental results, Kocher observed $10^6$ modular multiplication execution times ($a \cdot b \bmod n$) with random input on a 120-MHz Pentium computer running MSDOS. The result was approximately a normal distribution. It shows that the time consumption depends on operands $a$ and $b$. In addition, for 250 timing measurements he estimated the probability that subtracting the time for a correct iteration from each sample will reduce the total variance more than subtracting an incorrect iteration to be 84% for the first bit guess. Since the known bits become larger, the probability should improve [10].

There are two main ways to defeat a timing attack. First, we can perform a constant time operation in code sections that depend on the secret key [2]. A disadvantage of this approach is that time consumption is always the worst case. The second way is masking [13]. Here, random numbers are added to the cryptographic calculation that do not affect the result. This avoids dependencies between the key and the timing duration but works only for algorithms that have an algebraic structure to allow such a manipulation.

## 3   Related Work

There exists some work on the early analysis of fault injection [4,6,14,15]. However, they do not consider security threats that exploit physical emissions. There also exists a variety of work on the simulation of side-channel attacks, which are surveyed in [20]. However, to the best of our knowledge, none of the existing approaches proposes to model time and physical effects early in the development process. Instead, they focus on providing very detailed side channel information on the final implementation. In [5], attacks on smart cards are modeled in SystemC. However, they model a man-in-the-middle-attack and a DOS-attack and do not consider SCA. In [19], power attacks are simulated in SystemC. However, they do not consider timing attacks or other SCA. There exists an approach to analyze timing imbalance [12] and an approach which identifies timing disparate secure paths that could lead to information leakage through information flow analysis [11]. However, these approaches can not simulate attacks and only consider systems on register-transfer-level. In [9], the authors propose an approach for the evaluation and testing of timing attacks for a pass-code key breaker. However, the simulation and evaluation is done on the assembler level. With our SystemC based approach, we are targeting earlier phases of the development process, where only abstract models are available. Partial results of our work agree with [18]. Despite a different approach, they also came to the conclusion that side-channel security cannot be isolated at one abstraction level, and that it is important that physical simulation models at a high abstraction level accurately reflects the reality. They showed that minor differences in the power model can have a big influence on security assessment.

## 4   Modeling and Simulation of Kocher's Timing Attack

In this section, we discuss a SystemC model and simulation of the classical timing attack on the square-and-multiply algorithm [10]. To investigate which accuracy of modeling time is sufficient for the attack, we implement four different time

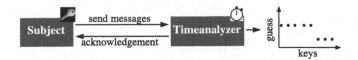

**Fig. 2.** Setup for the attack simulation

models with increasing accuracy. In the following, we present the general model, the four different time models and associated results. The SystemC model is licensed under GPL and freely available[1].

## 4.1  General Test Setup and Procedure

Our SystemC model consists of two modules, namely the attacker (*Timeana-lyzer*) and the subject that is attacked (*Subject*). An overview of the setup is shown in Fig. 2. The *Timeanalyzer* generates random messages and sends them to the *Subject*. The *Subject* then executes the decryption procedure using the square-and-multiply algorithm (see Fig. 1). To simulate time, we use SystemC `wait(t)`-statements, which delay the execution for t time units. In our model, we simulate the time consumption of all assignments and calculations. The *Timean-alyzer* saves the time spent per decrypted number and simulates the time of all guessed bits and the new guess bit (two possibilities) for each number, so that we get two different simulated times. Then, the variances discussed in Sect. 2 are calculated to determine the new bit. This process is repeated until the key has been completely guessed. In the setup, it is possible to perform this procedure not only for one key, but an interval can be specified in a header named *constants*, in which the described procedure is carried out for all numbers contained therein. In this way, we get an overview of which keys can be guessed successfully and which guesses fail. Furthermore, the modulo for the square-and-multiply algorithm, the number of messages sent per round, the number of bits guessed at the same time (one or two) and the time model variant can be specified in the header *constants*. Whether the key was guessed right or wrong and the wrongly guessed keys can be analyzed in a result chart.

## 4.2  Modeling Time

We have modeled the time consumption within the square-and-multiply algorithm in four variants:

1. **Time dependency on the input length.** In this variant, we assume that calculations with greater numbers take more time than with smaller numbers and that an assignment takes up constant time. Thus, the simulated time for each calculations depends on the length of the input in bits.

---

[1] https://www.uni-muenster.de/EmbSys/research/SysCSec.html.

```
                                          if(d[i] == 1)
                                          {
timeS = Utils::numberBits(s);                 timeX = Utils::numberBits(x);
                                              timeS = Utils::numberBits(s);
if((s * s) < n)
{                                             if((s * x) < n)
    s = s * s;                                {
    wait(timeS * 2, SC_PS);                       s = s * x;
}                                                 wait(timeS + timeX, SC_PS);
else                                           }
{                                             else
    s = (s * s) % n;                          {
    wait(timeS * 2, SC_PS);                       s = (s * x) % n;
    wait(MOD, SC_PS);                             wait(timeS + timeX, SC_PS);
}                                                 wait(MOD, SC_PS);
wait(ASSIGN,SC_PS);                           }
                                              wait(ASSIGN,SC_PS);
                                          }
```

**Fig. 3.** Instructions of the loop of the algorithm from Fig. 1 with assigned times

2. **Time dependency on intermediate results.** In this variant, we assume that the time of calculations depends on the length of both intermediate result $s$ and the input value $x$. Furthermore, we take into account that an additional subtraction is necessary if the intermediate result of the multiplication is greater than the modulus [7].

3. **Time dependency on the number of ones in intermediate results.** In this variant, we assume that more ones cause longer computations due to additional carry bits. Figure 3 shows the implementation of the loop body of the square-and-multiply algorithm with the assigned times and the case distinction for the modulo-operation. The number of ones is calculated using the method Utils:numberBits(bigint number). To simulate the time of a multiplication, the number of ones of the two operands is totaled.

4. **Time dependency refined by the Booth-algorithm.** In our fourth variant, the multiplication is implemented closer to hardware using the Booth-algorithm [3] for numbers in two's complement. The multiplication is carried out by shift operations, additions and subtractions, and we simulate the time of each single instruction. The time for the shift operation is constant, other calculations are dependent on the number of bits again.

### 4.3    Results and Improvements

We have evaluated our four time models with two different bit guess variants. First, with the classic procedure that only one bit is guessed and second with an extension designed by us where two bits are guessed.

*One Bit Guess.* This variant was carried out with the first three time models. The same results were always achieved for each variant in any test run. The guessed keys had almost always the structure $1 \ldots 10 \ldots 0$. With this approach, it was not possible to determine the order of the ones in the key. The results for Variant 1 for 500 messages and the key interval from 0 to 256 is shown on the top of Fig. 4. A higher number of 10000 messages led to the same result. We can see that two numbers, before the next power of two is reached, are guessed correctly, since the order of ones and zeros is not relevant here. Because of this, we got 241 errors. This phenomenon can be explained using the first time model and can be transferred to the subsequent ones. Let us consider the example with key 23 (in binary representation $10111_b$). The first step with the associated variance calculation is visualized on the left in Fig. 5. Each box symbolizes the simulation time for the displayed bit and a crossed-out bit means that the simulation time was subtracted. In the first time model the multiplication time is only dependent on the input size $x$. For this reason, all ones and all zeros have the same time consumption regardless of their position. For example, consider the length of the message to be processed is 10, giving a time consumption of 20 for every one and 10 for every zero. The total time that the *Timeanalyzer* measures during decryption is 90. Since the first digit of a number is always a one, the time for [1,0] and [1,1] is simulated in the first run and is subtracted from the measured time. For the guess 0, the exact time for the first two numbers of the correct key is subtracted and for the wrong guess 1, the leading 1 and the time of any other 1 are subtracted from the measured time because the time of the ones is not dependent on the position. The remaining time for guess 0 is the time consumed by three ones, thus 60. For guess 1, the resulting time with two ones and one zero is 50. For further messages, guess 1 will also result in a smaller resulting time than guess 0. When calculating the variance, there is therefore a smaller deviation for guess 1, so that this is assumed to be correct. Analogously, a one is always recommended for the following two bit guesses. When guessing the last bit, the time for the guess 0 is canceled with the measured time, so that there is no deviation and a zero is guessed in the last step. The resulting key is [1,1,1,1,0] and is a sort of ones and zeros. In the following two time models, time is also made dependent on the intermediate results, but it is still the case that guessing a 1 leads to a greater subtraction than guessing a 0. This results in smaller numbers and fewer deviations for a 1, so that this digit is assumed to be correct, although it is often not the case. For this reason, the other two result charts for Variant 2 and Variant 3 yield the same results and the key interval [0, 256] also results in 241 errors. This suggests that our time model does not meet Kocher's assumption that subtracting the time for a correct iteration from each sample reduces the total variance more than subtracting an incorrect iteration.

*Two Bits Guess.* To overcome the problem described above, we guess a bit by simulating two bits at once, calculate the corresponding variances again and use a modified query to decide whether to guess a zero or a one (see right picture in Fig. 5). As an example, consider key 23 again. First, the *Timeanalyzer* measures the time for the key and subtracts its simulated time. This consists of the simulation time of the leading one and two other bits. Thus, there are four cases for the later variance calculation. In the example, in case of [1,0,1], the measured time can be subtracted perfectly from the simulated time, so that only the measured time for [1,1] remains. In the other three cases, the simulated time of the numbers marked in green can also be subtracted perfectly from the measured time, but the numbers marked in red cannot. It should be noted that

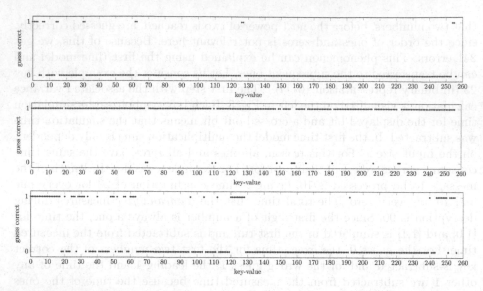

**Fig. 4.** Results for Variant 1 with one bit and for Variants 2 and 4 with two bit guess

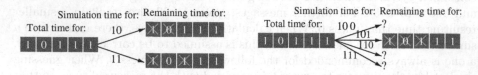

**Fig. 5.** Examples for the difference between total and remaining time

we only consider one of the last three time models, in which the time depends on the intermediate results. To decide whether we guess a 0 or a 1, we compare:

$$Var_{00} + Var_{01} < Var_{10} + Var_{11}.$$

This results in a larger deviation in case that a 1 is guessed because four simulated times ([1,0] and [1,1]) do not match the measured time and therefore lead to larger differences in deviation. Guessing two bits directly is not possible, since if [1,0,0] and [1,0,1] were compared, the same problem would arise as with the one bit guess. With this decision approach, we could see an improvement towards the one bit guess. The result chart for the second time model is shown in the middle of Fig. 4. Compared to the results with one bit (at the top of Fig. 4), we can see a clear improvement. In tests, we got 11 to 33 errors. A closer look at the errors reveals that almost all of them occur for the first two bit guesses. We achieved the best results with Variant 3. In tests, we got 0 to 3 errors per run with the same parameters as for Variant 2.

The last approach, by implementing the Booth-algorithm, results in a test in 193 errors for the key interval [0,256]. The results are shown on the bottom of Fig. 4. When we look at the errors, we see again a sorting by ones and zeros. We see that most correct guesses at higher numbers occur before a number, which is a power of two, is reached, because there the number of leading ones is very high and the last bits can be guessed correctly.

## 4.4  Discussion

Although Kocher's timing attack was difficult to model on a high level of abstraction, our simulation still worked after we improved the attack with the new bit guess method. We have succeeded in further developing Kocher's attack in the simulation environment. Variant 3 showed an improvement compared to Variant 2. The measurements by Kocher on the pentium-processor for the time of modular multiplication provide an indication of why the third time model works well. Kocher described the time for the modular multiplication in his results as an approximate normal distribution. In the third time model, we make the modular multiplication dependent on the number of bits in the operands. So each operand for the multiplication is binomially distributed and the sum of both operands is also binomially distributed which represents the time consumption. As a binomial distribution can be approximated by a normal distribution, this approach has the greatest similarity to Kocher's real measurements.

Variant 4 shows a significant deterioration compared to Variant 2 and Variant 3. It can be assumed that the higher effort in the multiply step no longer leads to a good correlation between data and time, since, for example, a binary representation with a lot of switches of ones and zeros causes a lot of time in the square step. It becomes clear that attacks are highly dependent on the hardware implementation. As a result, it is important to know at an early stage of development what the later hardware will look like in order to be able to abstract it for an accurate simulation that can find vulnerabilities. Since, as already mentioned, it is not clear where correlations between data and physical quantities come from, it is currently still difficult to simulate physical quantities in a meaningful way. There is also the danger that details are simulated in a more dominant way than they will be in the produced device. This would lead to false conclusions in an early security analysis.

## 5  Conclusion

In this paper, we have modeled and simulated the Kocher timing attack and the physical quantity time with increasing accuracy in SystemC to enable an early security analysis. We have created a test environment in which it was possible to simulate, to evaluate and to graphically represent these different approaches. We were able to show that the time for set bits in the private key is influenced too dominantly by our models. Through the simulation environment, we were able to identify this problem and modify the guess query of the attack. With the improvement, we were able to get different results for our time models. Variant 2 worked well and Variant 3 achieved even better results. We have shown that the model of Variant 3 corresponds most closely to reality (binomial distribution is similar to Kocher's measured values for modular multiplication), whereas the hardware-related Variant 4 achieved poor results.

We conclude that it is important to know how time values on the finished device will look like for operations that are being attacked to enable an early security analysis of SCA. An important result is that in the early design stage it is possible to simulate time in such a way that vulnerabilities can be identified in the manufactured device. The prerequisite, which is also a major difficulty, is that it has to be known in the early stage how operations are carried out by the hardware in later design phases and how this affects time consumption in order to be able to simulate approximated times in the early stage.

The above result also applies to other side-channel attacks, e.g. the power attacks modeled in [19]. There exists an *explanation gap*. The theoretical concept is designed by observing the physical quantity, but it is not yet well understood where the causal connection between the physical quantity and the data comes from. Thus, it remains an open challenge for future work how more elaborate physical effects that are exploited in SCA can be modeled early in the development process.

To solve the problem of the explanation gap, it appears appropriate to choose a similar approach to the simulation of the electromagnetic waves by designing a model through measurements. However, the model only applies to devices with the same design, since operations on different processors are optimized and implemented differently in hardware and thus have different emanations. Pipelining, out-of-order execution, parallelization and microcode also have an impact on physical quantity. For this reason, our assumptions for the time models are not universal for all processors. Due to the explanation gap, we were forced to make assumptions. Often, in different devices the same components are installed and the platform-based design is used. This does not only save costs and time, but could also offer the possibility of making devices more secure in the future if the manufacturer also creates a physical quantity simulation model of produced device components. These would have to be compatible and combinable with models from further components produced by other manufacturers. The approach could make more exact modeling possible in the future and improve the quality of models for physical quantities.

# References

1. Abrishamchi, M.A.N., Abdullah, A.H., Cheok, A.D., Bielawski, K.S.: Side channel attacks on smart home systems: a short overview. In: IECON 2017–43rd Annual Conference of the IEEE Industrial Electronics Society, pp. 8144–8149. IEEE (2017)
2. Barthe, G., Grégoire, B., Laporte, V.: Secure compilation of side-channel countermeasures: the case of cryptographic "constant-time". In: 2018 IEEE 31st Computer Security Foundations Symposium (CSF), pp. 328–343 (2018)
3. Booth, A.D.: A signed binary multiplication technique. Q. J. Mech. Appl. Math. 4(2), 236–240 (1951)
4. Burns, F., Murphy, J., Shang, D., Koelmans, A., Yakorlev, A.: Dynamic global security-aware synthesis using SystemC. IET Comput. Digital Tech. 1(4), 405–413 (2007)

5. Bushager, A., Zwolinski, M.: Modelling smart card security protocols in SystemC TLM. In: IEEE/IFIP International Conference on Embedded and Ubiquitous Computing, pp. 637–643, December 2010. https://doi.org/10.1109/EUC.2010.102
6. Chen, Y.Y., Hsu, C.H., Leu, K.L.: Analysis of system bus transaction vulnerability in SystemC TLM design platform. In: WSEAS International Conference. Proceedings. Mathematics and Computers in Science and Engineering, vol. 3. World Scientific and Engineering Academy and Society (2009)
7. Dhem, J.-F., Koeune, F., Leroux, P.-A., Mestré, P., Quisquater, J.-J., Willems, J.-L.: A practical implementation of the timing attack. In: Quisquater, J.-J., Schneier, B. (eds.) CARDIS 1998. LNCS, vol. 1820, pp. 167–182. Springer, Heidelberg (2000). https://doi.org/10.1007/10721064_15
8. IEEE: IEEE Standard for Standard SystemC Language Reference Manual. IEEE Std 1666-2011 (Revision of IEEE Std 1666–2005), pp. 1–638 (2012)
9. Kaur, S., Singh, B., Gupta, L.: Simulation-based method for analyzing timing attack against pass-code breaking system. In: Singh, P.K., Singh, Y., Chhabra, J.K., Illés, Z., Verma, C. (eds.) Recent Innovations in Computing. LNEE, vol. 855, pp. 795–808. Springer, Cham (2022). https://doi.org/10.1007/978-981-16-8892-8_60
10. Kocher, P.C.: Timing attacks on implementations of Diffie-Hellman, RSA, DSS, and other systems. In: Koblitz, N. (ed.) CRYPTO 1996. LNCS, vol. 1109, pp. 104–113. Springer, Heidelberg (1996). https://doi.org/10.1007/3-540-68697-5_9
11. Lai, X., Jenihhin, M., Raik, J., Paul, K.: PASCAL: timing SCA resistant design and verification flow. In: 2019 IEEE 25th International Symposium on On-Line Testing and Robust System Design (IOLTS), pp. 239–242. IEEE (2019)
12. Park, J., Corba, M., Antonio, E., Vigeant, R.L., Tehranipoor, M., Bhunia, S.: ATAVE: a framework for automatic timing attack vulnerability evaluation. In: 2017 IEEE 60th International Midwest Symposium on Circuits and Systems (MWSCAS), pp. 559–562. IEEE (2017)
13. Prouff, E., Rivain, M.: Masking against side-channel attacks: a formal security proof. In: Johansson, T., Nguyen, P.Q. (eds.) EUROCRYPT 2013. LNCS, vol. 7881, pp. 142–159. Springer, Heidelberg (2013). https://doi.org/10.1007/978-3-642-38348-9_9
14. Rothbart, K., Neffe, U., Steger, C., Weiss, R., Rieger, E., Mühlberger, A.: High level fault injection for attack simulation in smart cards. In: 13th Asian Test Symposium, pp. 118–121. IEEE (2004)
15. Rothbart, K., Neffe, U., Steger, C., Weiss, R., Rieger, E., Mühlberger, A.: An environment for design verification of smart card systems using attack simulation in SystemC. In: ACM/IEEE International Conference on Formal Methods and Models for Co-design (MEMOCODE), pp. 253–254. IEEE (2005)
16. Spreitzer, R., Moonsamy, V., Korak, T., Mangard, S.: Systematic classification of side-channel attacks: a case study for mobile devices. IEEE Commun. Surv. Tutorials 20(1), 465–488 (2017)
17. Stamp, M.: Information Security - Principles and Practice. Wiley, New York (2011)
18. Tiri, K., Verbauwhede, I.: Simulation models for side-channel information leaks. In: Design Automation Conference, pp. 228–233. IEEE (2005)
19. Treus, J., Herber, P.: Early analysis of security threats by modeling and simulating power attacks in SystemC. In: IEEE Vehicular Technology Conference, pp. 1–5. IEEE (2020)
20. Veshchikov, N., Guilley, S.: Use of simulators for side-channel analysis. In: European Symposium on Security and Privacy Workshops, pp. 104–112. IEEE (2017)

# Adaptation for Energy Saving in Time-Triggered Systems Using Meta-scheduling with Sample Points

Pascal Muoka[✉][iD], Oghenemaro Umuomo, Daniel Onwuchekwa,
and Roman Obermaisser

Institute for Embedded Systems, University of Siegen, Siegen, Germany
{pascal.muoka,daniel.onwuchekwa,roman.obermaisser}@uni-siegen.de,
oghenemaro.umuomo@student.uni-siegen.de

**Abstract.** Time-triggered systems offer significant advantages in embedded applications due to temporal predictability, implicit synchronisation and avoidance of resource contention. However, runtime adaptation of system services in these systems is motivated by energy efficiency without detriment to system performance. Too frequent adaptation result in more communication overhead. This work introduces a meta-scheduling technique with sample points to compute adapted static schedules for energy saving in time-triggered systems. An offline meta-scheduler optimises static schedules by applying slack events for energy saving at global periodic points in a schedule. The meta-scheduler maps the adaptation points to the runtime sampling period of adaptation. Slack events are reported synchronously by adaptation units at runtime, and adaptation is achieved through the aligned switching of component schedules facilitated by a Fault-Tolerant Agreement Protocol (FTAP). The meta-scheduler computes an MSG which holds all adapted schedules and describes the runtime switching of schedules based on reported slack events. The increased overhead due to periodic adaptation of the system schedule and energy saving of the meta-scheduling technique are evaluated. Results show a reduction in energy consumption compared with a base schedule while highlighting the trade-off between increased communication overhead and energy-saving.

**Keywords:** Energy saving · Communication overhead ·
Meta-scheduling · Adaptation · Time-triggered systems · Agreement
protocol

## 1  Introduction

Embedded system designers are increasingly faced with the demand for performance and dependability of embedded architectures in industrial automated

This work has received funding from the ECSEL Joint Undertaking (JU) under grant agreement No 877056. The JU receives support from the European Union's Horizon 2020 research and innovation programme and Spain, Italy, Austria, Germany, France, Finland, Switzerland.

systems to fulfil real-time requirements using less energy. Such energy saving must be achieved without detriment to system performance and dependability. Due to their determinism, embedded time-triggered (TT) architectures are beneficial for safety-critical applications and require runtime adaption for energy savings [1–3]. Energy expended due to the execution of application tasks by processing elements (PES) in the system dominates the energy consumption of TT systems. Existing energy-saving approaches use power/clock gating, which degrades system performance [4]. To maintain real-time constraints, performance requirements, and energy savings, adapted system schedules and power/clock gating are used.

TT systems use static time-triggered schedules to execute tasks and route communications while avoiding timing conflicts. TT static schedules are computed at development time for temporal predictability and resource contention avoidance without dynamic arbitration. However, these systems save energy by switching active system schedules to adapted static schedules [1]. Static schedules ensure that all application tasks meet their deadlines. Furthermore, overestimating tasks' worst-case execution time (WCET) leads to MPSoC under-utilisation at runtime, creating gain times [5]. A task's gain time is the difference between its completion and WCET. In this work, gain times, referred to as slack events, are excess runtime computational periods of PEs guaranteed in a system schedule for executing application tasks.

Existing methods for utilising slack events use task remapping, or meta-scheduling [1,6,7]. A meta-scheduler computes adapted static schedules for runtime slack events. Adapted schedules are organised in a multi-schedule graph (MSG) and saved in the TT system's memory during runtime. The MSG is used at runtime to switch the active system schedule when slack events are reported and agreed on [8]. Unfortunately, this technique suffers from a state space explosion problem, exponentially increasing the number of computed adapted schedules and the memory needed to store the MSG at runtime.

Nevertheless, the adapted schedules and process for active schedule switch must preserve system temporal predictability, implicit synchronisation, and resource contention avoidance to achieve adaptation without introducing system failures. For consistent and aligned runtime adaptation, active system schedule switching is performed deterministically through an interactive consistency protocol (ICP) [9], instantiated synchronously by MPSoC adaptation units to agree on reported slack events. The ICP is frequently instantiated to minimise slack reporting delay. Although it minimises this delay, increased system sampling increases the number of adaptation messages exchanged between the adaptation units for a given system schedule.

This work examines the increased communication overhead caused by too frequent runtime invocations of a fault-tolerant agreement protocol (FTAP) in a double-ring topology. We propose a meta-scheduler that maps the FTAP adaptation points to a base schedule. These points, referred to as sample points, are used by the meta-scheduler to compute adapted schedules for all reported slack events. The proposed technique identifies an optimal sample period for each system schedule as a trade-off between energy savings and communication overhead.

This paper continues as follows. Section 2 discusses related works. Next, Sect. 3 describes the proposed approach to runtime adaptation, the agreement protocol to establish a global system state, and a GA-based energy-saving meta-scheduler. Section 4 describes the experimental setup, and results are discussed in Sect. 5. Finally, Sect. 6 summarises the main contributions and findings.

## 2  Related Work

Sorkhpour et al. and Lenz et al. [6,8] proposed an offline meta-scheduler for adaptive time-triggered systems. Meta-scheduler takes an application, platform, and context model and computes a multi-schedule graph (MSG). The MSG determines the next system schedule given the reported runtime slack event. In both works, the MSG size was a concern due to the storage constraints of time-triggered systems. However, their meta-scheduler did not consider an optimal sample period for adaptation while computing adapted schedules to maximise energy-saving and minimise communication overhead.

Lenz et al. [9] proposed an interactive consistency protocol for global runtime adaption. Local context events are synchronously broadcasted to adaption units in a ring-topology. All adaption units require an agreed system context for an aligned schedule switch. In their work, the increased communication overhead due to multiple invocations of the agreement protocol was not considered.

Fafoutis et al. [10] used static adaptive scheduling in Time Slotted Channel Hopping (TSCH), a MAC protocol that allocates time slots in static schedules to nodes. Under-allocation of time slots causes packet loss and poor energy efficiency, while over-allocation improves performance but wastes energy. Over-allocation and runtime adaptation save energy and support traffic bursts. This approach does not consider the communication overhead of the agreement protocol. Paterna et al. [11] proposed runtime adaptive task allocation for ageing systems. Their technique balances performance and energy usage to fulfil deadlines. A closed-form linear programming approach combined with approximate offline solutions is used online to extend the target MPSoC's lifetime.

Our work analyses the increased communication overhead resulting from frequent FTAP invocations for fine to coarse granularity. We combine the FTAP timing in meta-scheduling and compute an offline MSG for energy savings. This technique trades energy savings for runtime communication overhead.

## 3  Proposed Approach

An aligned system schedule switch is used to achieve energy-saving in time-triggered embedded systems without detriment to performance. Dynamic slack is utilised to start future tasks earlier, where runtime sampling of the system status results in reported slack events. Adapted system schedules utilising dynamic slack for energy-saving are computed offline to guarantee real-time requirements while avoiding timing conflicts in computing and switching schedules.

## 3.1   Adaptation in Time-Triggered Multi-core Architectures

The time-triggered (TT) multi-core system architecture includes a network-on-chip (NoC) to facilitate message communication between PEs. The NoC's 2D-mesh topology connects PEs with bidirectional router links. PEs are instantiated as application cores in a homogenous architecture for executing tasks. Message-based ports offer an interface between the PEs and other components of the architecture, as illustrated in Fig. 1.

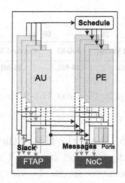

**Fig. 1.** Time-triggered Multi-core Architecture with Adaptation Unit

A static schedule prevents resource contention and maintains system synchronization through a global time base. Offline scheduling ensures tasks are completed before deadlines and messages through the NoC do not collide. The schedule allocates jobs and messages to system resources temporally, spatially, and contextually. Each task in the schedule is allocated to a PE and has a start time, WCET, and deadline. In addition, messages have injection times and an NoC routing path from source to destination.

Each PE in the TT system is connected to an adaptation unit (AU), which monitors tasks scheduled for the PE, as shown in Fig. 1. For tasks completed earlier than scheduled, a slack event is reported to the AU, which is the time difference between a task's worst-case execution time (WCET) and its execution time (ET) given by Eq. 1.

$$slack = WCET - ET. \tag{1}$$

A crash event is reported when a PE can not execute a task. This work exploits only slack events for energy efficiency. When a slack event is reported, the active schedule is dynamically switched to a static energy-efficient schedule that uses the slack time to execute future tasks earlier than previously scheduled, generating idle time at the end of the schedule. Idle times are used to reduce energy usage by power/clock-gating the system. Due to the difficulties in estimating task execution time, WCETs are allocated pessimistically at design time resulting in runtime slack events. An offline meta-scheduler computes a multi-schedule graph (MSG) for runtime slack events. Each system application cycle begins at the MSG root node, where no event is reported, and the system schedule is reset to the base schedule. MSG governs runtime schedule switching by considering the active node and the edge (slack event) to the next node.

The AU has a context monitor, a context agreement unit (CAU) and a schedule dispatcher. In addition, the AU is TT and scheduled independently to monitor and adapt the system schedule. The context monitor reports slack events to the CAU at scheduled times by encoding key identifiers of the event in a context bit string $lcontext_l$ illustrated in Fig. 2.

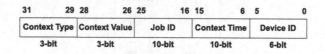

**Fig. 2.** Context Bit-String

In Fig. 2, *Device ID* and *Job ID* are the IDs of the local PE and scheduled task that originated the slack event. *Context time* is the system scheduling instant when the context monitor observes slack. *Context Value* represents the slack time compared to the tasks WCET given by Eq. 1, and *Context Type* denotes a slack event.

All AUs are aligned for all schedule switches to prevent resource contention, message collision in the TT system, and system failure resulting from a loss of synchronisation. In addition, all AUs are aligned using a fault-tolerant agreement protocol (FTAP), where the reported slack event $lcontext_l$ is collected from the context monitor and sent to all CAUs for agreement. ICP is extended to FTAP to prevent NoC bandwidth overloading and to improve its fault tolerance, where all AUs are connected in a double-ring topology and reported slack events are broadcast and received in both directions. The schedule dispatcher holds the MSG and determines the following system schedule based on the active schedule and agreed slack event *gcontext*. The active system schedule and observed slack event are used as a mask to extract the following system schedule, which is dispatched based on the AU schedule.

## 3.2   Context Agreement

CAUs synchronously instantiate FTAP to avoid schedule switch-related system failure. FTAP broadcasts all reported slack events to all CAUs through their dedicated ports, as illustrated in Fig. 1. Active schedule switching requires a consistent view of the system state represented by *gcontext*. FTAP ensures all CAUs have the same system state view, enabling the schedule switch.

FTAP duplicates reported slack events $lcontext_l$ into $lcontext_{l1}$, $lcontext_{l2}$ and broadcasts them to neighboring CAUs through the double-ring network. When $lcontext_{l1}$ and $lcontext_{l2}$ are relayed to the origin CAU, FTAP converges. FTAP compares $lcontext_{l1}$ to $lcontext_{l2}$ ensuring each duplicate bit is identical, converging them into $gcontext$ such that:

$$gcontext = \begin{cases} lcontext_l; & lcontext_{l1} = lcontext_{l2} \\ 0; & otherwise \end{cases} \qquad (2)$$

Algorithm 1 shows the FTAP pseudocode, where $lcontext_r$ represents a slack event from a CAU. $lcontext_{l1}$ and $lcontext_{l2}$ from the double-ring network are abstracted to $lcontext_l$. Each CAU relays all received slack events $lcontext_r$ until $lcontext_r = lcontext_l$. Each broadcast of a context bit-string $lcontext_r$, represented as a message $msg_x$ from one CAU to the next, is recorded as a hop $H_b$. The number of messages $Tmsg$ broadcasted per instance of FTAP is given by Eq. 3.

---

**Algorithm 1:** Fault-tolerant Agreement Protocol

**Input:** $lcontext_l$
**Output:** $gContext$

1   **if** *scheduled time* **then**
2     $lContext$ = Input from context monitor;
3     $gContext \oplus lcontext_l$;
4     broadcast $lcontext_l$ to next neighbour;
5     $lcontext_r = lcontext_l$ from neighbour;
6     **while** $lcontext_r \neq lcontext_l$ **do**
7       $gContext \oplus lcontext_r$;
8       broadcast $lcontext_r$ to next neighbour;
9       $lcontext_r = lcontext_r$ from neighbour;
10    **end while**
11 **else**
12    idle;
13 **end if**

---

$$Tmsg = H_b * N_{au}, \qquad (3)$$

where $N_{au}$ is the number of AUs in the TT system. $Tmsg$ represents the number of context bit-strings exchanged by the CAUs in each instance of the FTAP. FTAP is scheduled periodically to minimise the delay between reporting slack events and the schedule switch. Multiple instances of FTAP increase the number of context bit-strings exchanged by the CAUs given by Eq. 4. $C_{ov}$ is the total number of context bit-strings exchanged by the CAUs and represents the communication overhead of FTAP for a given system schedule period and FTAP frequency. A scheduled period is the time between the start of a schedule and the completion of the last task. *nSampPts* represents the number of instances of FTAP for a given system schedule.

$$C_{ov} = Tmsg * nSampPts. \tag{4}$$

## 3.3   Meta-scheduling with Sample Points for Adaptation

An offline meta-scheduler computes energy-efficient schedules at periodic points for reported runtime slack events. These sample points map online FTAP timing to offline meta-scheduling. Globally applied sample points ensure consistent schedule adaption and mapping of FTAP timing to meta-scheduling.

Meta-scheduler guarantees temporal constraints by fixing the parent schedule scheduling decisions before each sample point. This approach prevents resource contention while computing an energy-efficient schedule where future tasks are executed earlier. The meta-scheduler computes schedules $S_i$ utilising an application, platform, and context models (CM). Each computed schedule is a node in the multi-schedule graph (MSG). An edge in the MSG is a slack event for which an optimised child node is computed from the parent node.

The AM is a model of the runtime application represented as a tuple $<T, M>$. Each vertex $j_i \in T$ is an application task. $m_{i,k} \in M$ is a task-to-task message, as shown in Fig. 3. $<WCET, D>$ represents a task's worst-case execution time and deadline. A message $m_{i,k}$ is a tuple $<S, R, M_{sz}>$ where $S$ and $R$ are the sender and recipient tasks and $M_{sz}$ is the message size.

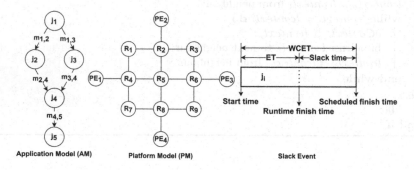

**Fig. 3.** Application Model, Platform Model and Slack Event

The PM represents the TT multi-core system and is modelled as an undirected graph $G_p$ represented as a tuple $< N, L >$. A vertex is either a PE $PE_i \in C$ for the execution of tasks or a router $R_i \in V$ to facilitate the exchange of messages between the PEs such that $N = C \cup V$. An edge $l \in L$ represents the bidirectional physical link of the TT multi-core system interconnecting all routers and PEs. The set of routers and their physical interconnect constitutes the NoC which has a 2D-mesh 3X3 topology.

The CM is a list of runtime slack events represented as a tuple $<j_i, sl_t>$ where $sl_t$ is the slack time of task $j_i$ expressed by Eq. 1. The meta-scheduler generates a multi-schedule graph (MSG) using the AM, PM and CM. The MSG is a directed graph of schedules which are the nodes of the graph, and slack events describe the edges of the MSG. Schedules are dispatched during runtime based on the active node in the MSG and the reported slack event.

The proposed meta-scheduler uses a genetic algorithm (GA) to compute a new schedule. The GA's objective function is to minimise the schedule makespan and maximise energy saving where idle times are used for power/clock gating. The GA's objective function ensures all computed adapted schedule maintains performance requirements while maximising energy saving. Initially, a base schedule $S_0$ is computed for a given AM and PM when no event is reported, and scheduling decisions are not decided. Then, the base schedule $S_0$ is added to the MSG as the root node, and a calendar of events $Cal$ is created from the CM and $S_0$ as described in Algorithm 2. The calendar of events $Cal$ details the reported times of all slack events $sl_t \in$ CM.

---

**Algorithm 2:** Meta-scheduling Procedure

---

   **Input:** $AM, PM, CM$
   **Output:** $MSG$
1  initialise $MSG$;
2  $S_0 = GA(AM, PM, V_d)$;
3  add $S_0$ to $MSG$;
4  $Cal =$ create calendar $(CM, S_0)$;
5  **Call Algorithm 3**;
6  **return** $MSG$

---

At each sample point, the meta-scheduler checks for the occurrence of slack events and replace their occurrence time with the sample point time. The difference between slack occurrence time and the sample point time, $\delta$, represents a delay in slack reporting, leading to a reduced slack time. The meta-scheduler ignores a slack event observed after the $WCET$ of its task and is not reported as it is no longer beneficial for adaptation. The $\delta$ and number of ignored slack events are minimised by increasing the frequency of FTAP, leading to increased overhead.

Scheduled WCET of jobs in the AM $WCET$ are replaced with the sample point time based on the reported slack events. Then, as described in Algorithm 3, a new schedule is computed from the updated AM $AM'$. The active schedule $S_i$ is used to fix decision variables $V_d$ before the sample point in the new scheduling problem. The decision variables consist of task allocation to PEs, task start times, message routing through the NoC, and message injection times. Finally, Algorithm 3 is recursively called with the updated models and calendar, the new schedule and MSG.

---

**Algorithm 3:** GA-based Meta-scheduler

---
**Input:** $AM$, $PM$, $Cal$, $S_i$, $MSG$
**Output:** $MSG$

1 **if** $Cal$ *is empty* **then**
2    | return
3 **else**
4    | $sl_t, sl_u, \ldots, sl_z$ = all events in $Cal$ before next sample point;
5    | $Cal'$ = remove $sl_t, sl_u, \ldots, sl_z$ from $Cal$;
6    | **Call Algorithm 3**($AM$, $PM$, $Cal'$, $S_i$, $MSG$);
7    | $AM'$ = apply $sl_t, sl_u, \ldots, sl_z$ to $AM$;
8    | fix decision variables $V_d$ $\forall$ $j_i, m_{ik}$ before each sample point;
9    | $S_i = GA(AM', PM, V_d)$;
10   | add $S_i$ as node and $sl_i, sl_k, \ldots, sl_n$ as edge to $MSG$;
11   | $Cal''$ = update $Cal'(S_i)$;
12   | **Call Algorithm 3**($AM'$, $PM$, $Cal''$, $S_i$, $MSG$);
13 **end if**

---

## 4 Experimental Setup

A time-triggered multi-core node is set up to observe the communication overhead of FTAP for different timing granularities. Then, these timing granularities are mapped to the meta-scheduler to compute adapted energy-saving schedules.

### 4.1 Time-Triggered Multi-core Architecture

The MPSoC architecture illustrated in Fig. 1 was instantiated using VHDL in the programmable logic of the Zynq UltraScale+ MPSoC ZCU102 Evaluation Kit. Four ARM-based processing cores were interconnected through a TTNoC [12]. Adaptation units were instantiated using the Vivado toolchain for each core in the MPSoC.

To evaluate the performance of FTAP, we simulated a schedule of 20 and 100 tasks with hard deadlines on the TT MPSoC architecture. Various timing granularity of FTAP in the range 100 μs to 500 μs was applied, and the communication overhead due to the exchange of slack events was observed. 100 μs represents a more frequent execution of the FTAP than 500 μs. The communication overhead criterion was chosen as it reflects the effectiveness of FTAP as a broadcast protocol. For each simulation of a schedule on the TT MPSoC, the total communication overhead was evaluated as the number of context bit strings $lcontext_r$ exchanged between the adaptation units. Assuming constant energy dissipated in the exchange of each context bit string, energy saving is achieved through an offset between energy saving from meta-scheduling and the total communication overhead due to instances of FTAP.

The total communication overhead $C_{ov}$ resulting from multiple instances of FTAP is given by Eq. 4. $nSampPts$ represents the number of instances of FTAP for a given schedule.

## 4.2   Meta-scheduler with Sample Points

Tasks are scheduled based on their WCET to ensure sufficient computational slots for completing tasks. This pessimism in scheduling tasks results, on average, in 70% of application tasks completed in 50% of their WCET [13]. The difference between a tasks completion time and its scheduled WCET gives its slack time given by Eq. 1. This slack time constitutes a slack event of the task and is described in the context model (CM). MSGs are therefore computed for slack events of 50% slack time due to the difficulty in offline estimation of runtime task execution times. The size of the CM is also limited to 10 slack events to evaluate the meta-schedulers energy saving.

The meta-scheduler was implemented in C++ using a GA-based scheduler [14,15]. The GA is set to a population size of 3000 and a number of generations of 200, resulting in better scheduling solutions. In addition, probabilities of crossover and mutation are set to 0.4 and 0.01, respectively, preventing a random search of the GA. Experiments were conducted using the OMNI computing cluster of the University of Siegen [16] for an AM consisting of 20 and 100 tasks and messages, with average WCETs between $700\,\mu s$ and $1000\,\mu s$. The PM is implemented as a 4-core $3 \times 3$ NoC mesh platform connected in a cross topology. The CM consists of 10 reported slack events distributed over tasks in the AM. The AM and PM are generated using the SNAP library [17].

To evaluate the impact of timing granularity of FTAP, we computed MSGs with sample points with granularity in the range $100\,\mu s$ to $500\,\mu s$. The chosen range ensures that all tasks in every schedule are sampled for a slack event at least once in a scheduled period, and sufficient time is available to adapt the schedule based on the reported slack event.

Energy efficiency is estimated as the percentage difference in makespan between the base schedule in a computed MSG and the last schedule (idle time), representing a path in the MSG from the root node to the leaf node. Idle times are utilised at runtime to power/clock gate the system, saving energy that would have been expanded in executing the application.

## 5   Results and Discussion

In Figs. 4a and 4b, we show the energy consumption of adapted schedules of the meta-scheduler. For each leaf schedule in the MSG, the makespan is compared to the makespan of the base schedule. For example, a 100% energy consumption indicates no reduction in the leaf schedule makespan, whereas a 50% energy consumption is characterised by a leaf schedule makespan half of the base schedule makespan. The energy consumption of the leaf schedule is evaluated for the timing granularity of FTAP in the range $100\,\mu s$ to $500\,\mu s$ for AMs with 20 and 100 tasks. The difference in the energy consumption of the adapted schedule to the base schedule represents the energy saved by switching to the adapted schedule.

The energy expanded in executing application tasks dominates the energy consumption of the system compared with the energy expanded in exchanging messages between agreement units. Therefore, the system's energy consumption reduction is observed when more slack events are adapted. An increase in FTAP frequency leads to overutilisation of the adaptation network bandwidth, thus increasing communication overhead. The communication overhead increases with a decrease in the sample period. Similarly, the meta-scheduling algorithm with sample points resulted in higher energy saving of the adapted schedules with a sample period of finer granularity. A key point in Fig. 4a, $\approx 180\,\mu s$, indicates a balance between the energy consumption and communication overhead. A decrease in the sample period from this point, although resulting in higher energy consumption, increases the communication overhead of FTAP. Conversely, an increase from this point results in lower energy saving and communication overhead. This result is also observed in Fig. 4b, where the key point is $\approx 270\,\mu s$.

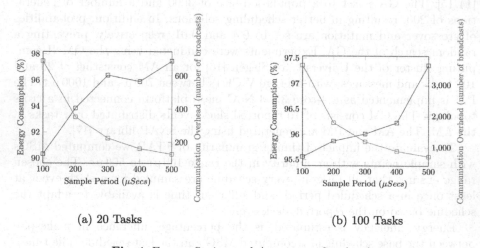

(a) 20 Tasks                              (b) 100 Tasks

**Fig. 4.** Energy Saving and Agreement Overhead

An increase in the density of reported slack events, $\rho$ results in increased energy saving observed by comparing Fig. 4a with Fig. 4b. In Fig. 4a, 10 slack events reported for 20 tasks, $\rho = 50\%$, results in $\approx 10\%$ energy saving compared with Fig. 4b where $\rho = 10\%$ results in $\approx 5\%$ energy saving. For each combination of the AM, PM, and CM, an optimal sample period can be selected to maximise energy saving while minimising the communication overhead of FTAP.

## 6    Conclusion

This work investigated the energy saving of time-triggered adapted schedules due to the periodic execution of a Fault-tolerant Agreement Protocol (FTAP) in an adaptive time-triggered multi-core architecture. Constraints such as communication overhead was considered in determining an optimal sample period for a given application. The periodic runtime execution of adaptation is mapped to a meta-scheduler's schedule generation. Schedules are adapted for energy saving, and the number of static schedules computed for runtime adaptation is observed. The meta-scheduler computes adapted schedules for slack events reported before each sample point as a result of superimposing runtime timing of FTAP on meta-scheduling. An optimal sample period for a given application scenario is determined as a trade-off between energy saving, communication overhead and the number of schedules needed for adaptation.

# References

1. Obermaisser, R., Ahmadian, H., Maleki, A., Bebawy, Y., Lenz, A., Sorkhpour, B.: Adaptive time-triggered multi-core architecture. Designs **3**, 7 (2019)
2. Heilmann, F., Syed, A., Fohler, G.: Mode-changes in COTS time-triggered network hardware without online reconfiguration. SIGBED Rev. **13**, 55–60 (2016)
3. Fohler, G., Gala, G., Pérez, P.-G., Pagetti, C.: Evaluation of DREAMS resource management solutions on a mixed-critical demonstrator. In: 9th European Congress on Embedded Real Time Software and Systems (ERTS) (2018)
4. Gaillardon, P., Beigne, E., Lesecq, S., Micheli, G.: A survey on low-power techniques with emerging technologies: from devices to systems. ACM J. Emerg. Technol. Comput. Syst. **12**(2), 1–26 (2015)
5. Audsley, N.-C., Davis, R.-I., Burns, A.: Mechanisms for enhancing the flexibility and utility of hard real-time systems. In: 5th IEEE RTSS, pp. 12–21 (1994)
6. Sorkhpour, B., Murshed, A., Obermaisser, R.: Meta-scheduling techniques for energy-efficient robust and adaptive time-triggered systems. In: IEEE 4th International Conference on Knowledge-Based Engineering and Innovation (KBEI), pp. 0143–0150 (2017)
7. Zou, Y., Pasricha, S.: HEFT: a hybrid system-level framework for enabling energy-efficient fault-tolerance in NoC based MPSoCs. In: International Conference on Hardware/Software Codesign and System Synthesis (CODES+ISSS), pp. 1–10 (2014)
8. Lenz, A., Pieper, T., Obermaisser, R.: Global adaptation for energy efficiency in multicore architectures. In: 25th Euromicro International Conference on Parallel, Distributed and Network-Based Processing (PDP), pp. 551–558 (2017)
9. Lenz, A., Obermaisser, R.: Global adaptation controlled by an interactive consistency protocol. J. Low Power Electron. Appl. **7**, 13 (2017)
10. Fafoutis, X., Elsts, A., Oikonomou, G., Piechocki, R., Craddock, I.: Adaptive static scheduling in IEEE 802.15.4 TSCH networks. In: IEEE 4th World Forum on Internet of Things (WF-IoT), pp. 263–268 (2018)
11. Paterna, F., Acquaviva, A., Benini, L.: Aging-aware energy-efficient workload allocation for mobile multimedia platforms. IEEE Trans. Parallel Distrib. Syst. **24**(8), 1489–1499 (2013)
12. Ahmadian, H., Obermaisser, R., Abuteir, M.: Time-triggered and rate-constrained on-chip communication in mixed-criticality systems. In: Proceedings of the 10th IEEE International Symposium on Embedded Multicore/Many-core Systems-on-Chip (MCSoC), pp. 117–124 (2016)
13. Axer, P., Ernst, R., et al.: Building timing predictable embedded systems. ACM Trans. Embed. Comput. Syst. (TECS) **13**(4), 82 (2014)
14. Wall, M., Galib, A.: A C++ Library of Genetic Algorithm Components. Mechanical Engineering Department Massachusetts Institute of Technology, Boston (1996)

15. Muoka, P., Onwuchekwa, D., Obermaisser, R.: Adaptive scheduling for time-triggered network-on-chip-based multi-core architecture using genetic algorithm. Electronics **11**, 49 (2022)
16. Universität Siegen. https://cluster.uni-siegen.de/omni/. Accessed 2 July 2022
17. Leskovec, J., Sosič, R.: SNAP: a general-purpose network analysis and graph-mining library. ACM Trans. Intell. Syst. Technol. **8** (2016)

# Communication Layer Architecture for a Production Line Digital Twin Using Hierarchical Colored Petri Nets

Adam Sulak, Charles Steinmetz[⊠], and Achim Rettberg

Hochschule Hamm-Lippstadt, 59557 Lippstadt, NRW, Germany
adam.sulak@stud.hshl.de, {charles.steinmetz,achim.rettberg}@hshl.de

**Abstract.** Modern enterprises must adapt to world events faster and faster to stay competitive. One of the ideas that gained traction in recent years that might help businesses speed up decision-making and decrease the cost of operations is the Digital Twin (DT) concept. Digital Twin allows for greater insight into how modelled systems work by creating a virtual copy of the system or object on which simulations can be performed. One of the key enablers to effective DTs is information exchange between the real system and its virtual copy. In this work we present architecture and prototype model of communication layer for Digital Twins of production line based on Hierarchical Colored Petri Nets (HCPNs).

**Keywords:** Digital Twin · Petri Net · Vertical Farm

## 1 Introduction

Modern factories are immensely complex systems of interconnected machines that have to meet stringent requirements of efficiency and reliability [5]. Any time a production line is stalling due to a machine failure or overproduction there is a significant cost being incurred. To avoid stalling and ultimately decrease the final cost of a manufactured good many managerial, logistical and technological advances have been made [6]. In the technological sphere those improvements usually came down to the automation of tasks that were previously performed by human factory workers.

There is still a lack to be filled in the automation of decision-making of complex systems. For instance, people who manage production lines have to constantly make decisions related to the maintenance and running of a production line that could be automated. In this context, this work-in-progress paper addresses the communication problems that arise when connecting a real production line with an intelligent management system. The proposed approach uses the concept of Digital Twin supported by Hierarchical Colored Petri Nets [9].

© IFIP International Federation for Information Processing 2023
Published by Springer Nature Switzerland AG 2023
S. Henkler et al. (Eds.): IESS 2022, IFIP AICT 669, pp. 41–50, 2023.
https://doi.org/10.1007/978-3-031-34214-1_4

# 2   Related Works

This chapter presents related works that have been used to build the proposed approach.

## 2.1   Place as a Physical Input

A paper published by researchers from Technical University of Crete presents an application of a Petri net based digital twin for controlling the process of creating an electric car from its design stage to the finished vehicle [8]. The Petri net in the DT uses extensions introduced in their previous work [7] as a way to describe unavoidable delays between specific tasks. This mechanism allows for creating a Digital Twin of the process which knows when to generate tokens depending on the stage of production.

## 2.2   Petri Net as a Messenger Between AI and the World

Researchers from Guangdong Institute of Semiconductor Industrial Technology and Northeastern University in their paper introduces new highly modified a version of Petri Net called Modified Hybrid Stochastic Timed Petri Nets (M-HSTPN) [2]. These nets define different types of places for modeling discrete, continuous, timed, and stochastic processes which allow for precise representation of complex phenomena within machinery.

The author's goal is to create a system for automatic fault detection using machine learning techniques. To do so they model machine processes as a Petri Nets whose places are affected by sensor outputs from the machine. The state of the entire Petri Net is then read by a Machine Learning model which can determine the next optimal state of the Net and enable suitable tokens.

# 3   Concept of Communication Layer Architecture for a Digital Twin Using Hierarchical Colored Petri Nets

## 3.1   Digital Twin

For our purposes, Digital Twin [4] is a virtual copy of a physical entity that is connected with that physical entity. The Digital Twin gathers information from the physical entity and uses that information to further improve the simulation accuracy of a real object. Digital Twin can contain components such as a precise 3 dimensional model of components of the real object, data about properties of materials being used, software representing internal logic of the device, database for data collection, analytics engine for interpretation of data and simulations, and optionally AI for making decisions [1].

In this paper, the focus is on the communication scheme for exchanging data between real production line machines and their Digital Twin.

## 3.2   Layer Architecture

Layer architecture (Fig. 1) is a basic view of the structure of interactions between the real and digital twin. The Device Layer includes all the physical devices within a production line. Those various status messages are received by Control Layer whose purpose is to translate them into one standard format that is readable to Decision Layer. The Control layer has to translate messages in the opposite direction. When Decision Layer sends information on what actions to perform next, Control Layer must translate those actions into messages specific to machinery on production line. The Decision Layer itself, as the name suggests, is responsible for aggregating information from Physical Twin and making decisions based on that information and historic data acquired by the Decision Layer over the lifetime of the entire system.

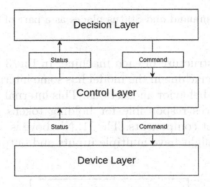

**Fig. 1.** Layer Architecture

**Control Mechanism for the Devices.** All the singular machines and interactions between them are modeled as HCPNs. The communication relies on a simple idea of having command and status places. These places are exposed as an interface to the outside world and allow a control of internal processes within a device. Command place is always an input place of a some transition that represents a state change while Status place is always an output place of a transition which informs about a change in the state. Figure 2a shows how this relation looks in practice. Places 'P_IN' and 'P_OUT' represent some physical inputs and outputs of the machine while 'CMD' and 'STS' ports are just abstract places for passing relevant information. The result of a transition is in the following Fig. 2b.

**Machines as Substitution Transitions.** Substitution Transition is a mechanism for creating reusable components and submodules in HCPNs. To utilize transition substitution within machines and production lines we first have to

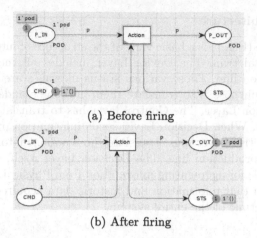

(a) Before firing

(b) After firing

**Fig. 2.** Command and Status places as a part of transition

identify the common structure of each machine. In Fig. 3 we have a model of a generic machine. Any machine in the model has some internal HCPN representation that models state behavior and actions. This internal Petri net has exposed input and output places responsible for holding tokens representing physical objects such as product components. The '1..N' above is a shorthand signifying that in fact machine might have multiple inputs and outputs.

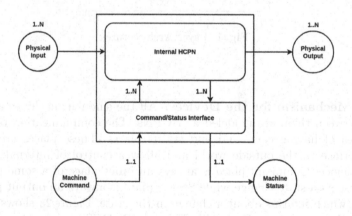

**Fig. 3.** Generic Machine Model

The second vital part is a Command/Status interface which takes a single machine command token from the control system and decomposes it to a set of command tokens for specific command places within an interface that connects to transitions in internal HCPN. The interface does the opposite when it comes to status messages. Status tokens received from internal HCPN are composed of a single status message inside the interface and exit a machine as a single machine status token. Internal HCPN and Command/Status interface form a single Petri which in higher level modeling is presented as a single transition between inputs and outputs.

**Control Places Types.** The following section we make a distinction between different types of command and status places. Those are:

- Transition Level Places - those are command and status places that are directly connected to transition within an internal process of a machine. Tokens in those places do not contain hierarchical data that can be decomposed.
- Machine Level Places - those are places that are connected to the entire machine represented as a substitution transition. Tokens in those places either contain a set of commands or statuses that can be later decomposed into individual transition-level tokens. Machine-level tokens additionally will include information that will help the machine interface to decompose it into transition-level tokens.
- Line Level Places - those are places that connect to the entire production line as a substitution transition. Line level places hold tokens that contain a set of data that is decomposable into individual Machine Level tokens which in turn can be further decomposed to Transition level tokens. Line Level tokens besides holding data for lower-level tokens also includes information about the destination place.

**Connecting Machines.** Chaining machines is done by sharing the output place of one machine with the input place of the other machines. Joined output and input places must have a matching place type.

Figure 4 shows how individual machines can be connected using physical places and form a production line.

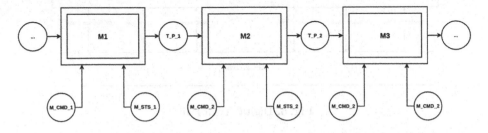

**Fig. 4.** Machine chaining pattern

Machines are substitution transitions (by convention substitution transitions have double border) that have a defined number of places for interacting with them. Those places are used as joining nodes in a higher-level design where the inner workings of the machine itself are not a concern.

**Network Bridge.** Network Bridge is an abstraction over all communication protocols involved in sending token values between the production line and digital twin inside the control layer. Network Bridge exposes Machine Command output and Machine Status input places to which individual machines can be connected, as well as input places for Line Commands and output places for Line Statuses. Tokens that go through those inputs and outputs are transformed into packets and moved over physical network to their destination which is either a real production line or Control Layer. Network Bridge is meant to rely on existing communication protocols and is not further explored in this work.

**Digital Twin and Decision Layer Interface.** The last section of the Control Layer consists of Status and Commands places for connecting to a Network Bridge, a pair of digital twins of a productions line, interfaces for reading and writing tokens and interfaces for interacting with the digital twins. How those elements are connected together is presented in Fig. 5.

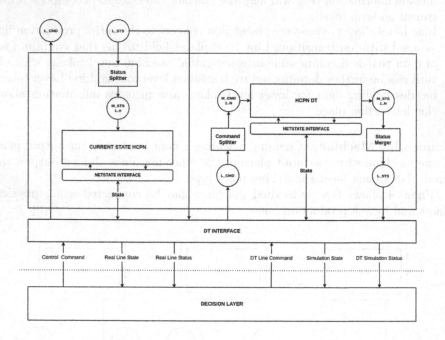

**Fig. 5.** Digital Twin Pair

The reason for having two digital twins in the control layer is because they serve different purposes. The first digital twin on the left side of the figure is used as a source of absolute truth for the Decision Layer.

The second location is the Main Interface which unpacks data from the token and passes it to Decision Layer.

The second digital twin in the right portion of the figure is dedicated to performing simulations. It is not interacting directly with the real production line, but it is used by Decision Layer in combination with historic data from the Knowledge Graph to determine the next Line Command token.

The advantage of having two Digital Twins is the fact that it enables the Decision Layer to detect unusual behaviors of the line by seeing differences between the output of the simulation and the actual state of the production line after sending the Command message. This way Decision The layer can compensate Digital Twins imperfections by informing human operators to investigate the issue or add compensation functions into the Knowledge Graph and use them when making future predictions.

## 4    Use Case Implementation: Vertical Farming

As a point of reference we use a concept model of a fully automated Vertical Farm [3]. The entire process relies on the movement of a special drawer-like containers called pods which are used as a vessel for growing plants. When plants are fully grown all the pods are being loaded to a lorry or other transporter and delivered to a food store. Empty pods come back to a facility to be reused.

A subprocess that will be used as an example for the control layer model is the simple the procedure of taking empty pods into a facility and preparing them for the next harvesting cycle (Fig. 6).

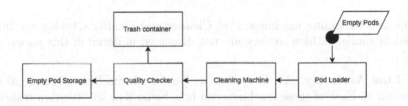

**Fig. 6.** Pod Cleaning and storage process

Each rectangle in the figure represents a machine within a facility and a black point with a rhomboid is an entry point of the process. The process here does not join elements together it only moves pods from one machine to the other which makes it an easy target for the first basic model.

### 4.1    Real Line

The first major component of the Control Layer is the net representation of the real production line which we refer to simply as 'Real Line'. Real Line is a chain of net models of each machine in the production line. Chaining is done by representing those nets as substitution transitions in a higher level assembly as presented earlier in Fig. 4. Real Line is built out of three sub-components: Pod Loader, Pod Cleaner and Quality Checker.

**Pod Loader.** Pod Loader is a machine through which delivery trucks can return empty pods to the Vertical Farm. The machine takes pods from the loading frame to which trucks unload empty containers and moves them into a temporary storage area. From that storage space pods can be moved further for cleaning and inspection if needed. In Fig. 7 we can see the CPN model of a Pod Loader which in following section is reduced down to a single substitution transition.

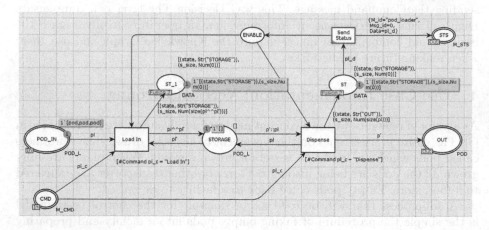

**Fig. 7.** Pod Loader model

The two remaining machines, Pod Cleaner and Quality Checker are implemented in similar fashion so they are not discussed in detail in this paper.

**Real Line Assembly.** At this point, we have each machine of the Real Line implemented. Each of these machines can now be used as substitution transition in the Real Line assembly. Figure 8 shows the Real Line model which very closely reflects the concept of machine chaining from Fig. 4. Places between substitution transitions are referred to as transition places because they are at the same time output machine on the left and the input of the machine on the right. They exist only to conform to the semantics of Petri nets. The physical inputs and outputs of the entire module are just inputs of the first machine in the line and outputs of the last machine in the line. Each machine also exposes Control Machine Level places for connecting to a Network Bridge.

### 4.2 Digital Twin Pair

Digital Twin is the last component of the Control Layer to which the Decision Layer has direct access through the Digital Twin Interface. DT Pair is also a component in which Petri Nets must expose an interface for direct manipulation of the twin network. This means CPN Tools is not a sufficient modeling tool for testing interactions with Decision Layer. However, this is not an obstacle

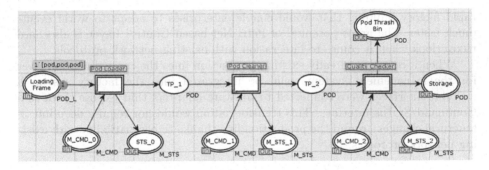

**Fig. 8.** Real Line model

when testing the Control Layer with a predetermined set of commands. DT Pair consists of two major assemblies, Current State DT and Simulation DT.

Current State Digital Twin (CSDT) uses a modified copy of the Real Line in which the state of the machine is altered according to the received status message and not a command. Machines in Current State DT is changed in such a way that their state transitions do not depend on external factors. What this means in practice is that any machine in which the processed object can take more than one path based on the parameters that are not controlled by the said machine is a subject of necessary modifications of the DT model so that external factors that affect state changes are replaced with paths that depend on the value of Machine Status Token. Simulation DT is an exact copy of the Real Line model. Main DT Interface connects to Line Level Places and Netstate Interface to allow data exchange with the Decision Layer.

Assembly of DT Pair closely reflects structure of DT Pair concept in Fig. 5. As with the initial concept DT Pair exposes one input which leads Line Status Messages to Status Splitter that distributes data to CSDT components and one output Line Command place which has a direct link to the Decision Layer. The missing connections of input and output places and Netstate Interfaces of the Digital Twins with the Main DT Interface are caused by the fact that CPN Tools are not built to model interactions between Petri Nets and other software. Netstate and DT interfaces are just commented annotations to show how other components fall in together.

## 5   Conclusion

This work has addressed the communication problems that arise when connecting a real production line with an intelligent management system. The approach has been developed based on the Digital Twin concept and supported by Hierarchical Colored Petri Nets.

Concept of Machine Chaining could find its applications in a new generation of production line design tools where machine manufacturers would provide their machine model as a form of closed-source API. This would open the door to rapid factory building that would enable enterprises to adapt to world events much faster. The great potential of Petri Net-based Control Layer is also hard to overlook when it comes to integration with existing network protocols.

When it comes to already existing production lines the communication layer for the management system could be integrated into the factory system if machine interfaces were connected to software adapters that expose them as a Command/Status interface. This transformation would not require deep infrastructural changes around the production line thanks to compatibility with existing network protocols.

# References

1. Aerospace Industries Association (AIAA). Digital Twin: Definition Value (2022). https://www.aiaa.org/docs/default-source/uploadedfiles/issues-and-advocacy/policypapers/digital-twin-institute-position-paper-(december-2020).pdf. Accessed 30 Mar 2022
2. Cao, R., et al.: A decision-making framework of hybrid system based on modified hybrid stochastic timed Petri Net and deep learning. IEEE Syst. J. **15**(2), 1804–1814 (2021). https://doi.org/10.1109/JSYST.2020.2983044
3. Despommier, D.: The Vertical Farm: Feeding the World in the 21st Century. Macmillan, New York (2010)
4. Grieves, M.: Digital twin: manufacturing excellence through virtual factory replication (2014). http://www.apriso.com
5. Lazarova-Molnar, S., Mohamed, N.: Reliability assessment in the context of Industry 4.0: data as a game changer. Procedia Comput. Sci. **151**, 691–698 (2019)
6. Souza, M.L.H., et al.: A survey on decision-making based on system reliability in the context of Industry 4.0. J. Manuf. Syst. **56**, 133–156 (2020)
7. Tsinarakis, G.J.: Modeling task dependencies in project management using Petri Nets with arc extensions. In: 2018 26th Mediterranean Conference on Control and Automation (MED), pp. 84–89 (2018). https://doi.org/10.1109/MED.2018.8442472
8. Tsinarakis, G.J., et al.: Implementation of a Petri-Net based digital twin for the development procedure of an electric vehicle. In: 2020 28th Mediterranean Conference on Control and Automation (MED), pp. 862–867. IEEE (2018)
9. Yang, Y., Tan, Q., Xiao, Y.: Verifying web services composition based on hierarchical colored Petri Nets. In: Proceedings of the First International Workshop on Interoperability of Heterogeneous Information Systems, pp. 47–54 (2005)

# Hardware Architectures for Embedded Systems

# Exploiting Heterogeneity in PIM Architectures for Data-Intensive Applications

Rafael Fão de Moura$^{(\boxtimes)}$ and Luigi Carro

Informatics Institute - Federal University of Rio Grande do Sul - Porto Alegre,
Porto Alegre, Brazil
{rfmoura,carro}@inf.ufrgs.br

**Abstract.** The scaling of common architectures for data-intensive applications is limited by the memory wall issues that culminate in energy and performance losses. Near-data or Processing in Memory (PIM) approach has been revisited to tackle this problem, along with a wide variety of architectural designs. However, these devices commonly rely on Application Specific Integrated Circuit (ASIC) designs, which in turn fail to cover the heterogeneity found in such applications. This paper discusses and exploits the heterogeneity present in the data-intensive realm by using a range of permutations for the tuple (algorithm, dataset, programming language). Relying on commonplace hardware performance metrics, we show how to identify the main changes in the processing demands and select the best near-data configuration. Using the proposed strategy, one could see a performance difference of 1.52x, and an Energy Delay Product of 2.86x in the studied examples.

**Keywords:** Data-intensive applications · Near-data · Heterogeneous processing

## 1 Introduction

Today's hardware and software industries have witnessed rapid growth in the realm of data-intensive applications. The processing of Neural Networks (NNs), data science, and the Internet of Things (IoT) inhibits both the scaling and the straightforward adoption of common architectures, giving their high energy consumption and slowdown, and unexploited performance potential. Such energy and performance losses are caused by the massive off-chip communication and data movements performed along the memory hierarchy. For example, up to 59% of the total processing time of the NN AlexNet and 81% of the polybench suite are spent in the cache hierarchy [7,20].

Hence, and in addition to the constraints imposed by the end of Dennard scaling and Moore's law [5], computer architects are required to develop solutions to extract performance providing the best speedup and energy savings for these modern application domains [21]. Alternatively, the concept of near-data processing

© IFIP International Federation for Information Processing 2023
Published by Springer Nature Switzerland AG 2023
S. Henkler et al. (Eds.): IESS 2022, IFIP AICT 669, pp. 53–64, 2023.
https://doi.org/10.1007/978-3-031-34214-1_5

or Processing in Memory (PIM) conceives a mature solution for this problem. By placing computing units closer to where the data resides and bypassing the memory bottleneck, the desired computing capabilities can be achieved. Thus, several near-data designs have been proposed, most of them relying on the specialization of Functional Units (FUs) for a specific group of algorithms [12].

Designing specialized hardware for algorithms undoubtedly provides the best gains, but lacks versatility and fails to cover the heterogeneity that the actual industry scenario may exhibit, especially when adding new variables to be optimized: the **dataset** and the **programming language**. Regarding the dataset, several algorithms are known to scale their processing demands according to the input size. As an example of this property, in the YOLOv3 NN, for inputs of $320 \times 320$, $416 \times 416$, and $608 \times 608$ pixels, this processing requires 39, 66, and 141 GFLOPS (Billions of Floating-Point Operations Per Second) [18], which configures a polynomial growth, but still predictable demand. However, heterogeneous demands appear in applications where the input data's meaning dictates the processing flow (i.e., graphs and pointer chasing, genomics, decision problems) [27].

When adding the programming language, a new horizon of possibilities and constraints opens. Targeting fast software development and a short Time to Market (TTM), according to Cass et al. [4], five out of 10 of the top programming languages of 2020 are interpreted or require a Virtual Machine (VM) to run, with the two most popular belonging for this class. Building ASIC accelerators for VMs is certainly a challenging task, since they are known to present a plethora of different operations. Looking only at how the two most used interpreted languages work (Java and Python), the Java bytecode's processing configures a stack machine, while Python bytecode follows a load-store-like architecture [8,24]. Hence, several approaches try translating the input application to a synthesizable version, such as the High-Level Synthesis (HLS) and Pynq tools [15]. However, such tools provoke several ruptures caused by the high-level language development cycle, since they cannot sustain the same generality and resources the original programming language offers.

The main **problem** that this paper tackles is to call attention to the heterogeneity found in the processing of current data-intensive applications. As our **goal**, we present clues on how to exploit these traits in the future of near-data architectures. By varying parameters in the tuple (algorithm, dataset, programming language), we collect and identify the hardware implementation possibilities that give us directions on choosing the best near-data configuration for the given iteration.

The following section presents an overview of state-of-the-art near-data architectures according to the FU type present in the design. Also, a discussion about the main features of performance and energy harvesting is made. Section 3 discusses heterogeneity found in data-intensive execution, and points out how future near-data engines could benefit from it. Following the related works, we select the most straightforward design that offers the best versatility for heterogeneous processing demands, and introduces the near-data architecture for data-intensive applications in Sect. 4. Section 5 describes the methodology used to compare the efficiency metrics of each scenario explored, and we explore the design space of the in-memory General Purpose Processor (GPP) and cache, and compile the results. Finally, Sect. 6 concludes the paper and enumerates the next steps of this work.

## 2   Background and Related Work

This section provides an overview of fundamental aspects and a description of state-of-the-art near-data architectures. As aforesaid, the main goal of performing computation closer to where the data resides is to exploit the smaller latency and higher memory bandwidth, which is internally available in the memory device. Regarding the integration model, most PIM designs rely on stacking custom logical fabric in a 3D-DRAM arrangement [1–3,23]. However, processing elements can also be placed at different levels of the memory hierarchy and combined with different memory technologies. Once several near-data designs have been proposed and studied, we follow the PIM categorization into three classes, as proposed by de Lima et al. [12] and illustrated in Fig. 1.

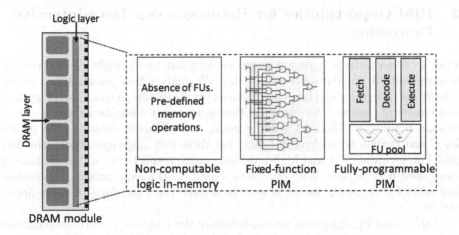

**Fig. 1.** Overview of different PIM classes

- **Non-computable logic in-memory:** As the name suggests, this class of PIM does not properly perform computation inside the main memory. Instead, logic in-memory is added to provide software-transparent operations, such as atomic and non-cacheable instructions. An example of this type of PIM is Micron's HMC, which incorporates a proper Instruction Set Architecture (ISA) to support several memory operations [16].
- **Fixed-function PIM:** This class encloses devices with pre-defined or fixed operations, which are established by custom logic design (ASICs) attached to the main memory, or even the organization or an intrinsic property of the memory. As their main feature, such PIM devices are tuned to compute an algorithm or a set of procedures, relying on the specialization of processing.

Hence, such an approach undoubtedly delivers the best gains in performance and energy. As an example of this approach, we refer to Zhuo et al. [27] that adopts ASIC accelerators coupled to a DRAM module to accelerate graph processing, and Wang et al. [25] that exploits intrinsic dot-product operations in an RRAM device to accelerate NNs. However, the two main drawbacks of this approach are the lack of versatility for general-purpose processing, and the disruption of software development and basic Operating Systems (OS) foundations.

- **Fully programmable PIM:** The last class comprises complete or simplified general-purpose processors with the basic blocks required to fetch, decode and execute instructions. Since these devices do not lean on the specialization of the processing, they harvest performance by lessening the memory wall effects due to the poverty of data locality. To represent this class, we refer to [6, 13, 17, 26]. The big advantage of this approach is its straightforward implementation, since it provides natural compatibility with SO and programming language resources.

## 3   PIM Opportunities for Heterogeneous Data-Intensive Processing

This section conducts a design space exploration to highlight the processing heterogeneity in the data-intensive realm. We analyze how permutations in the (algorithm, programming language, dataset) tuple dictate/impact overall system and hardware counters' performance. Hence, we select a few data-intensive algorithms, running a C and a Python version, over different datasets. The choice for C and Python stems from the fact that these two languages occupy the first position, regarding low and high-level languages, respectively, in the ranking of most used languages in 2020 [4]. Then, based on the experiments, we disclose heuristics for designing future near-data architectures for data-intensive applications.

Table 1 and Fig. 2 present a compilation of the system's performance metrics and execution time breakdown for different iterations. The algorithm's running was conducted on an Intel10500 GPP platform, coupled to an 8GB@2666MHz DDR4 DRAM. The applications chosen are the Breadth-First Search (BFS) and Page rank. BFS and Page rank's selection comprises two common ways of data representation and processing within the data-intensive realm: linked-lists management/pointer chasing (BFS), and matrix operations (Page rank). The tags *small* and *big* refer to the graph datasets mouse-retina-1 and twitter-higgs respectively, both extracted from [19]. Aiming to identify the guidelines to decide whether to execute a data-intensive application on a near-data architecture, we target hardware counters that reflect the overall performance (CPU cycles) and the memories' status (Prefetch hit ratio, Data-cache Level One (DL1) hit ratio, as DL2 and DL3 hit ratios).

**Table 1.** System's performance indicators for running different permutations of (algorithm, language, dataset).

| Algorithm | Language | Input size | CPU cycles (thousands) | Mem. inst.(%) | Prefetch hit(%) | DL1 hit(%) | DL2 hit(%) | DL3 hit(%) |
|-----------|----------|-----------|-----------|-----------|-----------|-----------|-----------|-----------|
| BFS | C | small | 524 | 40 | 32 | 92 | 53 | 35 |
| | | big | 747.499 | 41 | 20 | 73 | 34 | 43 |
| | Python | small | 4.925 | 49 | 46 | 99 | 63 | 82 |
| | | big | 55.880.176 | 60 | 24 | 88 | 11 | 99 |
| Page rank | C | small | 8.003 | 45 | 54 | 97 | 54 | 93 |
| | | big | 27.692.649 | 44 | 12 | 84 | 26 | 46 |
| | Python | small | 524.511 | 54 | 57 | 98 | 95 | 96 |
| | | big | 614.118.403 | 54 | 27 | 95 | 86 | 64 |

The main observations regarding the results are:

- Python applications spend more cycles on CPU and DL1, and perform a larger number of memory accesses than the C counterpart. This result suggests a higher demand for processing and more pressure over the memory system due to the VM's presence. In fact, according to Ismail et al. [9], up to 70% of the processing time of Python applications is spent running the VM's routines instead of the algorithm itself.
- The two leading indicators when increasing the input size are the CPU cycles, and the prefetch hit ratio. It is predictable to have more CPU cycles as we increase the input size. However, as a big dataset is used as input, the prefetch hit ratio drastically decreases. Such reduction may indicate poor data locality, reflecting a lower hit ratio on the cache levels.

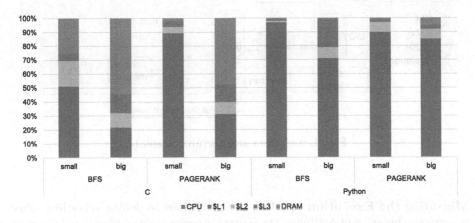

**Fig. 2.** Execution time breakdown for several (algorithm,language,dataset) permutations

It is possible to conclude that there exists heterogeneity in terms of processing demands in the data-intensive realm. One can observe that a single/one variable change of the experimented tuple leads to different time percentages spent on memories and CPU, but with contrasting behaviors. For example, to accelerate the Page rank algorithm over the big dataset, we do not need to put our efforts on the CPU or the DL1 cache. However, considering the same experiment, if we choose to run it on a Python VM, now CPU and DL1 are a bottleneck for the execution. Hence, an efficient design of future near-data engines must consider such algorithm, language, and size-related impacts, as will be presented in the following section.

## 4    Near-data Architecture for Heterogeneous Execution

As presented in Sect. 2, the Fully-programmable class of PIM offers the best tradeoff regarding versatility and performance. Hence, based on the opportunities for heterogeneous processing in data-intensive applications in Sect. 3, we select this class as the base for our PIM model. Figure 3 presents the PIM datapath to be explored in our design space exploration. As one can observe, the three main blocks that compose our design are a GPP host processor, the 3D-stacked memory arrangement, and the near-data processor built on the memory's logic layer.

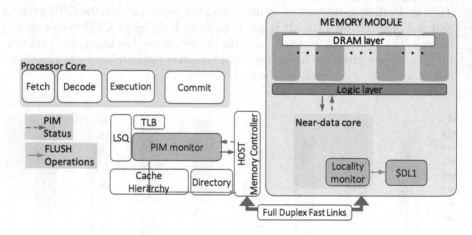

**Fig. 3.** Near-data architecture datapath

**Migrating the Execution to PIM.** Since we claim to deliver versatility allied to software/binary compatibility, the central premise of our design is to keep both host and PIM CPUs running under the same ISA. This decision relieves us of setting up an *offloading mechanism* to dispatch near-data instructions. Instead, our architecture moves the application's context along with the host-PIM pair.

The hardware component responsible for triggering and coordinating the migration of an application to the near-data processor is the *PIM monitor*.

The PIM monitor works by watching the host CPU's performance counters and evaluating whether the application can benefit from moving its execution to the near-data CPU. Relying on the experiments conducted in Sect. 3, the most straightforward way to determine the feasibility of near-data execution for a data-intensive application is based on the data locality diagnosis. Hence, we chose the memory's prefetch hit ratio as the metric to indicate such data locality. This approach simplifies the heuristic to choose whether to execute on the near-data CPU: *if the memory's prefetch hit ratio is less than a threshold, move the execution to PIM.*

Once the PIM monitor detects the near-data as the target processor, the following steps are performed to pair the host and near-data CPUs:

1. Host CPU flushes its pipeline.
2. Host and near-data CPUs synchronize their states by transferring all the physical register's values.
3. Data coherence protocol starts, as explained below.
4. The host CPU is set to a low-power state.
5. Near-data CPU starts processing according to the last Program Counter (PC)'s value.

**Keeping Data Coherent.** Keeping data coherence in PIM architectures must handle shared data between host processors, the cache hierarchy, and the main memory with its logic layer (where the near-data CPU resides). Since both the near-data and the host CPUs may have access to a shared memory region, traditional data coherence mechanisms (e.g., the MOESI protocol) are not enough for this task. Adopting current data coherence protocols entails heavy traffic of snooping messages, since the narrow communication channel between memories in the hierarchy may introduce losses for bandwidth and time. Thus, we opt to synchronize the host-near-data CPUs pair only during an application's migration to minimize overhead and keep data coherent throughout a fine-grain protocol. Hence, the PIM monitor coordinates all actions regarding data coherence at the third step of an application's migration, as indicated above.

The proposed data coherence management works: after the host CPU flushes its pipeline and synchronizes its state with the near-data pair, the PIM monitor sends a flush request to the first data cache level (DL1) for all the cache blocks having their dirty bit status set. All flush requests are transmitted from the DL1 and forwarded to the next cache level until they arrive at the main memory, where the requests are sent back to the PIM monitor. Inside each cache level, the flush requests are treated as lookups: if there is a cache block match, a writeback or an invalidate command is enqueued in the write buffer of the current cache level. One can notice that the proposed mechanism does not replace the role of current data coherence protocols. Hence, any existing cache coherence, such as MOESI, must be in charge of this task.

**Enabling VM Processing on PIM.** As Sect. 3 explored, applications that still present considerable levels of data locality may still benefit from near-data execution. Also, the high-level languages running on VMs reveal a particular case: the VM's data locality inhibits a straightforward (CPU directly coupled to the main memory) PIM adoption. Thus, as shown in Fig. 3, we add a DL1 to our near-data CPU to enable the VM execution on PIM devices. Similarly, as performed by the PIM monitor, the *Locality monitor* watches the DL1's hit ratio of the near-data CPU to decide whether to enable caching in the PIM execution. Likewise, *if the DL1's hit ratio is less than a threshold, the locality monitor performs flushes for all dirty blocks in the DL1 and turns it off.*

## 5    Experimental Setup and Results

### 5.1    Evaluation Setup

This section presents the methodology used to evaluate the near-data mechanism. To provide broad coverage for the design space exploration of (algorithm, language, dataset) tuple and a heterogeneous setup, we select several data-intensive algorithms, with C and Python implementations, running on big and small datasets. We pick the BFS, Page rank, Apriori, and CRISPR-CAS9 synthesis as algorithms. For the BFS and Page rank, we refer to the datasets mouse-retina-1 and Twitter-Higgs as the small and big datasets, respectively. Apriori algorithm runs the NYC Small Business Services dataset [14]. CRISPR-CAS9 uses the human genome (hg38), taken from [10].

**Table 2.** Hardware setup.

| Scenario | HW setup |
|----------|----------|
| Baseline | 8-issue@2 GHZ OoO RISCV CPU |
|          | 32 kB IL1/DL1 cache |
|          | 256 kB L2 cache |
|          | 16MB L3 cache |
|          | 8 GB DDR4@2666 Mhz DRAM |
| 2-issue PIM | 2-issue@2 GHZ OoO RISCV CPU |
|          | 32 kB IL1/DL1 cache |
|          | 8 GB DDR4@2666 Mhz DRAM |
| 8-issue PIM | 8-issue@2 GHZ OoO RISCV CPU |
|          | 32 kB IL1/DL1 cache |
|          | 8 GB DDR4@2666 Mhz DRAM |

Also, we synthesize two different Out-of-Order (OoO) configurations using the RISCV rocket chip generator [11]. Then, we set up two near-data CPUS comprising the 2-issue and the 8-issue CPUS with IL1 and DL1 caches, as described in Table 2. As the host processor and baseline for all the results, we refer to the 8-issue OoO, with $L1, $L2, and $L3. To accurate our simulation, we have implemented all the mechanisms mentioned in Sect. 4 on the NDA framework presented in [22]

## 5.2 Results

To support further evaluation of the two experimented near-data setups, we present in Table 3 a compilation of the hardware counters taken as indicators for the PIM monitor and Data locality blocks to decide whether to execute on near-data and caching the applications.

**Table 3.** Hardware counters compilation.

| Scenario | DL1 hit(%) | Prefetch hit(%) |
|----------|------------|-----------------|
| BFS_C:small | 92 | 32 |
| BFS_C:big | 72 | 20 |
| BFS_PY:small | 99 | 46 |
| BFS_PY:big | 99 | 24 |
| Page rank_C:small | 97 | 54 |
| Page rank_C:big | 84 | 12 |
| Page rank_PY:small | 98 | 57 |
| Page rank_PY:big | 96 | 27 |
| CRISPR_PY:big | 99 | 53 |
| Apriori_PY:big | 98 | 31 |

Figure 4 presents the speedup and the normalized Energy Delay Product (EDP) over the baseline for all the experimented scenarios. Regarding the 8-issue PIM scenario, which has the same CPU configuration as the baseline, one can observe speedup values ranging from 1.02x to 1.52x. In several cases, the most significant performance gains occur with the employment of big datasets, since these scenarios present poor data locality (Table 3) and benefit more from near-data execution. Further, changing the programming language from C to Python reveals a diminished but favorable acceleration. Compared to the C counterparts, the smaller speedup that Python scenarios present arises due to the necessity of a DL1 and the interpreter/VM's overhead.

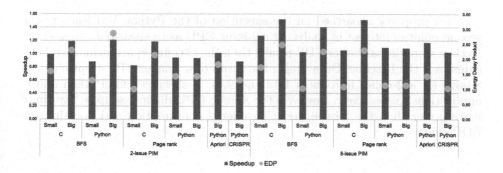

**Fig. 4.** Speedup and EDP for the experimented scenarios

Also, when examining the EDP results, gains vary from 1.03x to 2.48x. These results expose, on average, more expressive reductions in energy consumption than speedup. Such more significant energy reduction occurs due to the absence of the elevated levels of power dissipated in the intermediate cache levels along the memory hierarchy. Moreover, it is known that the SRAM cells composing current cache memories present a higher power density than DRAM and CPU's circuitry, leading to the results. Likewise, those scenarios with big datasets and C as the programming language present the most significant EDP improvements.

With the employment of a smaller (in terms of processing power), 2-issue OoO CPU in the near-data engine, two new points come to analysis: First, there is a noticeable reduction of the presented speedup values, sometimes leading to a slowdown (values less than one). The such slowdown can be expected, since we are decreasing the number of instructions the CPU can issue and execute by a factor of four times, on average. However, the most remarkable observation regarding performance is that Python's VM benefits better from a smaller CPU. To disclose such behavior, we present Fig. 5, which shows the average Cycles Per Instruction (CPI) metric for C and Python execution, when ranging the number of issues in the OoO processor.

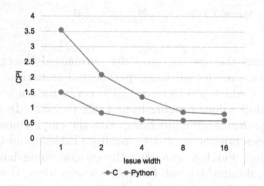

**Fig. 5.** Average CPI values for different issue sizes

Such property unearthed on the execution of the Python VM leads to the second point of interest in analyzing a 2-issue CPU as the near-data engine: the Python scenario has better EDP results than the C counterpart, achieving 2.86x gains over the baseline. On average, the setup of a smaller CPU (replacing the 8-issue for a 2-issue) introduces 1.4x and 2.6x of slowdown for Python and C applications, respectively. However, the 8-issue CPU dissipates up to five times more power than the 2-issue, reducing energy consumption and boosting the EDP gains.

# 6   Conclusion and Future Work

This paper presents and discusses the heterogeneity found in executing data-intensive applications. Through the design space exploration of (algorithm, language, dataset) permutations, we disclaimed how the dataset size and the employment of high-level interpret languages require different processing demands, thus raising opportunities for future near-data processing. Then, we built two near-data engines to run and adapt their execution by supporting on-the-fly processing requirements. Evaluation results reported EDP gains up to 2.86x, with Python applications benefiting from adopting smaller OoO CPUs. In future work, we intend to study heterogeneous CPUs inside a Big-Little approach to exploit high-level language demands for processing better.

# References

1. Ahn, J., Hong, S., Yoo, S., Mutlu, O., Choi, K.: A scalable processing-in-memory accelerator for parallel graph processing. In: Proceedings of the 42nd Annual International Symposium on Computer Architecture, pp. 105–117 (2015)

2. Alves, M.A., Diener, M., Santos, P.C., Carro, L.: Large vector extensions inside the hmc. In: 2016 Design, Automation & Test in Europe Conference & Exhibition (DATE), pp. 1249–1254. IEEE (2016)

3. Azarkhish, E., Rossi, D., Loi, I., Benini, L.: Design and evaluation of a processing-in-memory architecture for the smart memory cube. In: Hannig, F., Cardoso, J.M.P., Pionteck, T., Fey, D., Schröder-Preikschat, W., Teich, J. (eds.) ARCS 2016. LNCS, vol. 9637, pp. 19–31. Springer, Cham (2016). https://doi.org/10.1007/978-3-319-30695-7_2

4. Cass, S.: The top programming languages: Our latest rankings put python on top-again-[careers]. IEEE Spectr. **57**(8), 22–22 (2020)

5. Dennard, R.H., Gaensslen, F.H., Yu, H.N., Rideout, V.L., Bassous, E., LeBlanc, A.R.: Design of ion-implanted mosfet's with very small physical dimensions. IEEE J. Solid-State Circuits **9**(5), 256–268 (1974)

6. Drumond, M., et al.: The mondrian data engine. ACM SIGARCH Comput. Architect. News **45**(2), 639–651 (2017)

7. Gonçalves, L.R., Moura, R.F.D., Carro, L.: Aggressive energy reduction for video inference with software-only strategies. ACM Trans. Embedded Comput. Syst. (TECS) **18**(5s), 1–20 (2019)

8. Ike-Nwosu, O.: Inside the python virtual machine (2015)

9. Ismail, M., Suh, G.E.: Quantitative overhead analysis for python. In: 2018 IEEE International Symposium on Workload Characterization (IISWC), pp. 36–47. IEEE (2018)

10. Kent, W.J., et al.: The human genome browser at ucsc. Genome Res. **12**(6), 996–1006 (2002)

11. Lee, Y.: Risc-v "rocket chip" soc generator in chisel. In: Online slides (2015). https://riscv.org/wp-content/uploads/2015/01/riscv-rocket-chip-generator-workshop-jan2015.pdf

12. de Lima, J.P.C., Santos, P.C., Alves, M.A., Beck, A.C., Carro, L.: Design space exploration for pim architectures in 3d-stacked memories. In: Proceedings of the 15th ACM International Conference on Computing Frontiers, pp. 113–120 (2018)

13. Nair, R., et al.: Active memory cube: a processing-in-memory architecture for exascale systems. IBM J. Res. Dev. **59**(2/3), 1–17 (2015)
14. Okamoto, K.: What is being done with open government data? an exploratory analysis of public uses of new york city open data. Webology **13**(1) (2016)
15. O'Loughlin, D., Coffey, A., Callaly, F., Lyons, D., Morgan, F.: Xilinx vivado high level synthesis: Case studies (2014)
16. Pawlowski, J.T.: Hybrid memory cube (hmc). In: 2011 IEEE Hot Chips 23 Symposium (HCS), pp. 1–24. IEEE (2011)
17. Pugsley, S.H., et al.: Ndc: Analyzing the impact of 3d-stacked memory+ logic devices on mapreduce workloads. In: 2014 IEEE International Symposium on Performance Analysis of Systems and Software (ISPASS), pp. 190–200. IEEE (2014)
18. Redmon, J., Farhadi, A.: Yolov3: An incremental improvement. arXiv preprint arXiv:1804.02767 (2018)
19. Rossi, R.A., Ahmed, N.K.: An interactive data repository with visual analytics. SIGKDD Explor. **17**(2), 37–41 (2016). http://networkrepository.com
20. Santos, P.C., de Lima, J.P., de Moura, R.F., Alves, M.A., Beck, A.C., Carro, L.: Enabling near-data accelerators adoption by through investigation of datapath solutions. Int. J. Parallel Prog. **49**(2), 237–252 (2021)
21. Santos, P.C., Oliveira, G.F., Tomé, D.G., Alves, M.A., Almeida, E.C., Carro, L.: Operand size reconfiguration for big data processing in memory. In: Design, Automation & Test in Europe Conference & Exhibition (DATE), 2017, pp. 710–715. IEEE (2017)
22. Santos, P.C., et al.: Exploring iot platform with technologically agnostic processing-in-memory framework. In: Proceedings of the Workshop on INTelligent Embedded Systems Architectures and Applications, pp. 1–6 (2018)
23. Scrbak, M., Islam, M., Kavi, K.M., Ignatowski, M., Jayasena, N.: Exploring the processing-in-memory design space. J. Syst. Architect. **75**, 59–67 (2017)
24. Venners, B.: The java virtual machine. Java and the Java virtual machine: definition, verification, validation (1998)
25. Wang, Q., Wang, X., Lee, S.H., Meng, F.H., Lu, W.D.: A deep neural network accelerator based on tiled rram architecture. In: 2019 IEEE International Electron Devices Meeting (IEDM), pp. 14–4. IEEE (2019)
26. Zhang, D., Jayasena, N., Lyashevsky, A., Greathouse, J.L., Xu, L., Ignatowski, M.: Top-pim: Throughput-oriented programmable processing in memory. In: Proceedings of the 23rd International Symposium on High-performance Parallel and Distributed Computing, pp. 85–98 (2014)
27. Zhuo, Y., et al.: Graphq: Scalable pim-based graph processing. In: Proceedings of the 52nd Annual IEEE/ACM International Symposium on Microarchitecture, pp. 712–725 (2019)

# Demonstrating Scalability
# of the Checkerboard GPC with SystemC
# TLM-2.0

Yutong Wang(✉), Arya Daroui, and Rainer Dömer

CECS, University of California Irvine, Irvine, USA
{yutongw5,adaroui,doemer}@uci.edu

**Abstract.** With the growing complexity of embedded applications, system architects integrate more processors into System-on-Chip (SoC) designs. Since scalability of such systems is a key criterion for their efficiency, regular array-type architectures are preferred that can easily grow in size. In this work, we model in SystemC TLM-2.0 a Grid of Processing Cells (GPC) with a Checkerboard arrangement of processors and memories. To demonstrate its scalability, we evaluate the performance of a highly parallel Mandelbrot renderer on growing Checkerboard platforms. Our results confirm that the performance scales well with the number of processors.

**Keywords:** SystemC · Scalability · System-on-Chip Design · TLM-2.0 · Grid of Processing Cells (GPC)

## 1  Introduction

The Grid of Processing Cells (GPC) has been proposed as a regular system architecture of many cores with local memories that are arranged in a scalable 2-dimensional array with only local interconnect [6]. The "Checkerboard" variant places memories in between processing cores in alternating fashion, allowing processors to access only neighboring memories. While the proposed GPC platform intuitively appears scalable, its scalability has not actually been shown. In this work [19], we design a detailed Checkerboard GPC model and describe it in SystemC TLM-2.0 [2]. Our model is fully functional, scalable in width and height, and can accurately simulate timing and thus measure performance. For our performance and scalability analysis, we choose the visualization of the Mandelbrot set [14] as a suitable application, because it is a perfectly (embarrassingly) parallel program, and map it onto the processing cells of the Checkerboard GPC. In addition to detailed timing measurements with growing Checkerboard sizes, we also compare the performance to a theoretical model with perfect linear scalability to show that the Checkerboard model also scales well.

### 1.1  Background and Related Work

Many computer architectures have been proposed and used throughout the years. The classic von Neumann computer architecture [11] has one memory

© IFIP International Federation for Information Processing 2023
Published by Springer Nature Switzerland AG 2023
S. Henkler et al. (Eds.): IESS 2022, IFIP AICT 669, pp. 65–77, 2023.
https://doi.org/10.1007/978-3-031-34214-1_6

bus between the memory and the central processing unit (CPU). The original Harvard architecture [9] and its modern implementation, the modified Harvard architecture, all use a single shared memory bus. While modern computers are typically organized as symmetric multiprocessors (SMPs) [12], there is only a single shared memory connected via a bus interface. Having a single memory with a shared bus for CPU(s) severely limits the scalability of these architectures.

Knowing that the architectures with a single memory bus have a memory bottleneck, other architectures with better scalability have been proposed. The Raw architecture [15] is a 4 × 4 tiled architecture designed with multiple buses and multiple memories. It allows application-specific resource allocation and data flow within the chip. The tiled architecture of Raw also allows it to scale with increasing silicon density [15]. Another scalable architecture is the Tile Processor [20] [4]. The TILE64 and the TILEPro64 processor are both manufactured by Tilera. Both processors show the scalability of the tiled architecture. With each tile containing a general-purpose processor, a cache, and a router, TILE64 and TILEPro64 are able to communicate with each other and other I/O devices on a large 8 × 8 scale [1,16,17]. Intel's Teraflops Research Chip, codenamed Polaris, is another scalable many-core design with a network-on-chip architecture [18]. Polaris consists of a 10 × 8 2D mesh network (80 cores) with a sustained performance of 1.28 teraFLOPS, demonstrating very good scalability [13]. Intel's Single-Chip Cloud Computer (SCC) is another tiled platform that communicates through an architecture similar to a cloud computer in a data center. The chip contains tiles in a 4 × 6 2D-mesh with 2 P54C Pentium cores and a router in each tile. Intel hopes to make SCC scale to 100+ cores by having each chip communicate with another chip [8,10]. KiloCore processor array, which contains 1000 independent processors and 12 memory modules on a single chip, is another scalable tiled-like architecture with multiple memory buses [3]. Their data indicates that under most conditions, the processor array has a near-optimal proportional scaling of power dissipation.

While the aforementioned related tiled architectures offer a large degree of scalability, the Checkerboard GPC studied in this work [19] promises to scale better in the sense that each processing core has only access to local/neighboring memories (which restricts application size and poses a burden on programmability). Thus, the memory access speed is not influenced by the size of the grid. Regardless of where a core is located in the grid, it has constant access to its neighboring memories, making Checkerboard GPC truly scalable.

## 1.2   Problem Definition

The Checkerboard Grid of Processing Cells has been proposed in [6] but not implemented. There is a need for a simulatable model to demonstrate the viability of the proposed architecture. In this work [19], we design a SystemC TLM-2.0 model and map a perfectly parallel application to it. We compare our experimental results to a theoretical model to show that the Checkerboard GPC truly scales well.

## 2   The "Checkerboard" Grid of Processing Cells

In this section, we review the Checkerboard GPC [6] and present its implementation in SystemC TLM-2.0.

### 2.1   Overview of Checkerboard SystemC Model

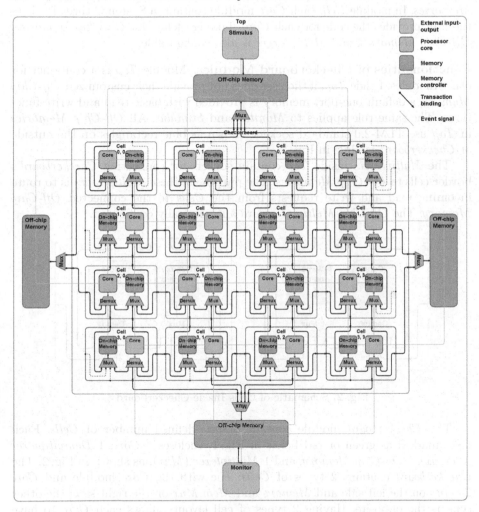

**Fig. 1.** Schematic of Checkerboard 4 × 4 GPC Model

**Checkerboard Model Components.** An example Checkerboard 4 × 4 model schematic is shown in Fig. 1. Our Checkerboard SystemC model contains many TLM-2.0 modules. The highest level module is named *Top*, and contains modules *Stimulus, Monitor, Off-Chip Memories, Multiplexers*, and *Checkerboard*. The *Checkerboard* module contains width by height *Cell* modules. Each *Cell* contains four modules, *Core, On-Chip Memory, Demultiplexer* and *Multiplexer*.

**Checkerboard Model Configuration.** In the *Top* module, modules *Stimulus, Monitor, Multiplexers,* and *Off-Chip Memories* are configurable. In *Checkerboard* module, the number of *Cells* can be configured based on need with two parameters, Grid Width and Grid Height. We built a Python-based code generator that takes Grid Width and Grid Height and generates the corresponding SystemC code [19]. The user can also limit the size of both *On-Chip* and *Off-Chip Memories.* In module *Cell*, each *Core* module contains a SystemC thread, where the user provides the code for each *Core.* Timing (delay) for *On-Chip Memories, Off-Chip Memories,* and *Multiplexers* is also configurable.

**Functionalities of Checkerboard Modules.** Module *Top* is a container for other modules. Inside *Top,* if the user does not provide their customized *Off-Chip Memory,* a default one-port memory is provided with basic read and write functions. The same rule applies to *Monitor* and *Stimulus.* All *Off-Chip Memories* in *Top* use TLM-2.0 standard sockets, shown as blue rectangles on the outside of *Checkerboard* module in Fig. 1.

The *Multiplexers* inside *Top* contain sockets for connecting *Checkerboard*'s border cells to *Off-Chip Memories.* The purpose of these *Multiplexers* is to route incoming read and write requests from the *Cells* to the connected *Off-Chip Memory.* The *Off-Chip Multiplexers* are automatically configured.

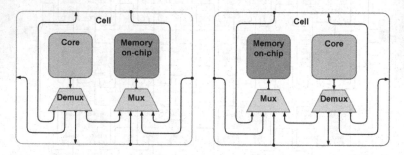

**Fig. 2.** Schematic of Cells Inside Checkerboard

The *Checkerboard* module contains a user-defined number of *Cells.* Each *Cell,* marked as green or red boxes in Fig. 1, encloses 1 *Core,* 1 *Demultiplexer (Demux),* 1 *On-Chip Memory,* and 1 *Multiplexer (Mux),* as shown in Fig. 2. The *Checkerboard* contains 2 types of *Cells:* one with the *Core* module and *Core Demux* on the left side and *Memory* and *Mem Mux* on the right side; the other type is the opposite. Having 2 types of cell layouts allows each *Core* to have access to 4 adjacent memories without crossing wires. A *Core* has only 1 socket, and it is connected to a *Demux.* The *Core's Demux* takes the request from that *Core* and forwards it to the 4 connected memories based on the address of the *Core* and the address of the payload. Each *Core* has its own SystemC thread. The user is in charge of providing the functionalities of each thread.

**Core-Memory-Core Communication.** The yellow lines that go across *Cells* in Fig. 1 are SystemC event signals used to notify nearby *Cores* about memory accesses. There is one event associated with each *On-Chip* and *Off-Chip memory*. This memory-event setup allows each *Core* to notify the events of neighboring memories and wake up nearby *Cores*, thus allowing safely synchronized *Core* to *Core* message passing.

**Checkerboard Address Space.** As described in Sect. 2.1, when a *Core* sends a read or write request to a specific memory address, the payload goes through the *Core's Demux*. The *Demux* forwards the payload to the correct memory based on the requested address and the sender's address.

| Bit | 31 | Address bits | Address bits | 31 - 2xAddress bits |
|---|---|---|---|---|
| On-chip memory | 0 | lg(height) | lg(width) | rest of address |
| Off-chip memory | 1 | pos | | rest of address |

**Fig. 3.** Memory Address for Checkerboard Model

As shown in Fig. 3, the most significant address bit is used to differentiate the *On-Chip* and *Off-Chip Memories*. For *Off-Chip Memories*, two more bits are needed to identify the four *Off-Chip Memories*. Address bits for *On-Chip Memories* depend on the number of bits needed to represent Grid Height and Grid Width of the Checkerboard. Each *Core* only uses its local address space, so the Checkerboard can truly scale to any size.

**Model Limitations.** The current version of Checkerboard uses a 32-bit address space. As Checkerboard grid grows in size, each *On-Chip Memory* has a smaller maximum size. This also limits the current Checkerboard to a maximum size of $16 \times 16$ *Cells*. In the future, we design a 64-bit address space or higher to allow even larger Checkerboards. The mapping of any application onto the Checkerboard is currently done manually, which is prone to human error and also time-consuming. We plan to automate this process.

## 3    Mandelbrot Set Visualization on Checkerboard

We now describe the parallel application chosen to demonstrate scalability. For a detailed definition of the Mandelbrot Set, please refer to the original documentation [14].

### 3.1    Theoretical Model of Mandelbrot Set Visualization

As a perfectly scalable reference we also build a Theoretical Mandelbrot Set Visualization model, theoretical model for short. The theoretical model is implemented with SystemC TLM-2.0 with accurate memory behavior.

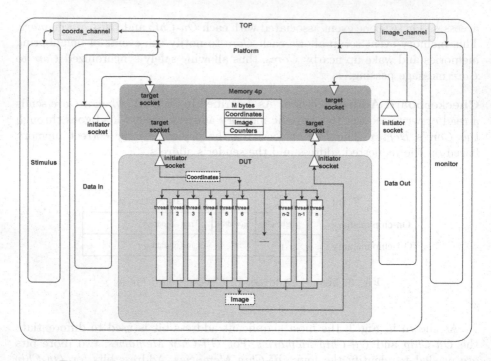

**Fig. 4.** Schematic of Theoretical Mandelbrot Set Visualization Model

**Overview of Theoretical Model.** As shown in Fig. 4, the highest level module that contains all submodules is named *TOP*. *TOP* contains module *Stimulus, Monitor, Platform*, and two communication *Channels*. Module *Platform* contains module *Data In, Data Out, four-port Memory*, and *DUT*.

*Stimulus* is in charge of creating the coordinates used for the Mandelbrot algorithm. The coordinates have a custom data structure with four floating point numbers that represent the top, left, right, and bottom bounds. Because each image requires a coordinate, the number of coordinates generated from stimulus equals the number of images. Each coordinate generated after the first one will be zoomed in based on a zoom factor. The zoom factor is user-defined and defaults to 0.7.

*Platform* contains module *Data In, Data Out*, and *DUT*. The module in charge of communication between *Stimulus* and *Platform* is a SystemC channel class. When a coordinate reaches *Platform*, it is received by the module *Data In*. *Data In* runs an infinite loop of sending coordinates right after receiving coordinates from *Stimulus*. Similarly, *Data Out* runs an infinite loop of sending images to *Monitor*. The purpose of *Data In* and *Data Out* is to represent I/O units.

Module *DUT* wraps all the Mandelbrot parallel units, as shown in Figure 4. The number of parallel units $n$ used is a preprocessor macro and can be power of 2 with a maximum of 256. Each parallel unit calculates $\lfloor \frac{height of image}{number of parallel units} \rfloor$ rows of pixels. If the height of the image is not divisible by $n$, the last parallel unit will compute the extra rows of pixels.

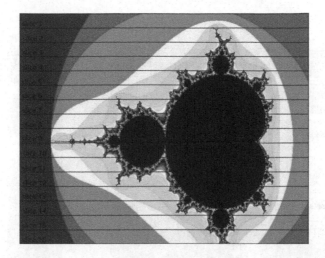

**Fig. 5.** Example of 640 * 512 Mandelbrot with 16 Parallel Units

All parallel units work on the same instance of image, as illustrated in Fig. 5. An image consists of three 2D array of values to store a pixel's red, green and blue intensity. Inside each thread, the function $f_c(z_{n+1})) = z_n^2 + c$ is executed in a loop to determine the number of iterations each pixel takes to breach the threshold. After getting the iteration number for a pixel, that number is mapped to a colored pixel on the image. After calculating and displaying all assigned pixels, the thread pauses and waits for the next coordinate to start the next image. When the entire image is filled, DUT sends the image to memory and reads the next coordinate. The Monitor is in charge of stopping the program when it receives the expected number of images.

### 3.2 Mapping on the Checkerboard Model

Figure 6 shows our mapping of Mandelbrot slices on each *Core* in the Checkerboard model. Each image is divided into *GridWidth* * *GridHeight* slices, and each *Core* in the mapped Checkerboard is in charge of 1 slice of the image. In this example, each black line in Fig. 6 represents a flow of 4 slices of the image.

The simplified dataflow of a single column of Mandelbrot on Checkerboard $4 \times 4$ is shown on the right of Fig. 6. A red block represents a *Core*, and a blue block represents a memory. Every *Core* uses the same functions: PopCoord(), PushCoord(), PopSlice(), and PushSlice(). PopCoords() takes the generated coordinates from the memory above that *Core*. If the *Core* is in the first row, then PopCoords() take the coordinate from *Off-Chip Memory*. Function PushCoords() pushes a coordinate to the local memory of that *Core*. PushSlice() function writes a finished image slice to a *Core*'s local *On-Chip Memory*, if *Core* is in the last row, then PushSlice() write to *Off-Chip Memory* at the bottom. PopSlice() reads a image slice from the memory of the Cell above.

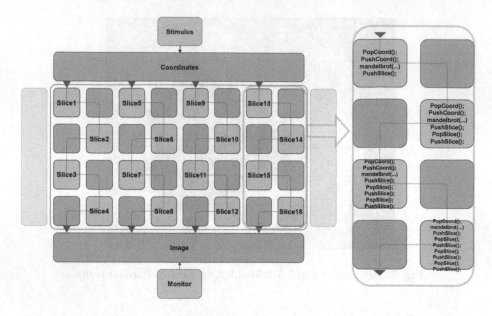

**Fig. 6.** Mapping of Mandelbrot slices on a Checkerboard 4x4 Model

When a *Core* receives a coordinate for Mandelbrot calculation, it forwards that coordinate to the next *Core*. That *Core* then starts the Mandelbrot calculation function. Once all the pixels in a slice are calculated, the *Core* pushes this slice to memory. For *Cores* that are not in the first row, the number of Pushing and Popping depends on the vertical location of that *Core*.

Module *Monitor* checks the bottom *Off-Chip Memory* for every write. It waits until every slice of the image is filled and then displays a message that an image has been completed. Once the number of images matches the specified number, *Monitor* terminates the simulation.

## 4   Experiments and Results

This section introduces our experimental setup and testing methodology for Mandelbrot Set Visualization on the theoretical model and on the Checkerboard model. All recorded results are in unit time since the actual timing delay for *On-Chip Memory*, *Off-Chip Memory*, *Multiplexers* and *Demultiplexers* is irrelevant[1] for our goal of showing scalability.

---

[1] Please note that the irrelevant timing delays do not include *contention* time when modules wait for access to shared bus resources. Contention is a very relevant criterion when comparing system architectures with shared resources and would be highly desirable in our comparison. However, measurement of contention was unfortunately not yet available in the described models at the time of the experiments reported in this section.

## 4.1 Experimental Setup

All experiments use the same parameters, the only difference is the number of parallel units. Experiments run for Mandelbrot Set Visualization use the following parameters: 576 Image Height, 640 Image Width, 4096 Max Iteration, 5 Images. All experiments are run on the same machine with fixed frequency of 3.4GHz. For repeatability we turn off all I/O functions and frequency scaling of the host. 1 computation unit time equals 1 iteration taken in the Mandelbrot Set calculation loop. 1 communication unit time equals 1 word read/write from/to the memory and 1 read/write request forwarded by the mux/demux.

## 4.2 Results and Evaluation for the Theoretical Model

We built and simulated the theoretical model in SystemC TLM-2.0. Here we report for an increasing number of parallel units (PU), the computation unit time (Comp UT), the communication unit time (Comm UT), the simulator run time (SRT), and improvement factor (IF). IF is calculated from $\frac{previousCompUT}{currentCompUT}$.

**Table 1.** Experimental Results for Mandelbrot Set Visualization Theoretical Model

| PU | Comp UT | Comm UT | SRT (sec) | IF |
|----|---------|---------|-----------|-----|
| 1 | 4075078882 | 1658988 | 18.45 | |
| 2 | 2543059511 | 1658988 | 18.85 | 1.602431585 |
| 4 | 1471609768 | 1658988 | 19.06 | 1.728080070 |
| 8 | 764406229 | 1658988 | 19.49 | 1.925167159 |
| 16 | 389276159 | 1658988 | 19.83 | 1.963660531 |
| 32 | 196793623 | 1658988 | 19.89 | 1.978093360 |
| 64 | 98881005 | 1658988 | 20.24 | 1.990206542 |

Table 1 shows the simulation results for the theoretical model. For a growing number of parallel units, the calculation time decreases almost proportionally while the communication time remains constant due to the single memory bus. Taking into account that the slices require a different number of iterations (slices in the middle of the image are more expensive to calculate), both observations match the expectation for the otherwise perfectly scalable model. The simulator runtime increases slightly, which is also expected as the simulator needs to manage more threads and has increasing context switching activity. The values of Table 1 are also plotted in Figs. 7 and 8 for comparison.

## 4.3 Results and Evaluation for the Checkerboard Model

Table 2 shows the simulation results for the Checkerboard model. The improvement factor in Table 2 is only calculated when number of PU matches Table 1. For a growing number of parallel units, the calculation time decreases proportionally while the communication time varies based on the layout. The observed calculation time matches our expectation for the same reason as in the theoretical model.

**Table 2.** Experimental Results for Mandelbrot on Checkerboard Model

| PU | Layout | Comp UT | Comm UT | SRT | IF |
|----|--------|---------|---------|-----|-----|
| 1 | $1 \times 1$ | 4075078982 | 1659029 | 18.61 | |
| 2 | $1 \times 2$ | 2543059611 | 829598 | 18.72 | 1.602431561 |
| 3 | $1 \times 3$ | 1799580598 | 553130 | 19.22 | |
| 4 | $2 \times 2$ | 1471609868 | 1106205 | 19.30 | 1.728080021 |
| 6 | $2 \times 3$ | 1001359981 | 553151 | 19.40 | |
| 8 | $2 \times 4$ | 748676317 | 553270 | 19.69 | 1.965615627 |
| 9 | $3 \times 3$ | 677227735 | 430285 | 19.87 | |
| 12 | $3 \times 4$ | 513788640 | 530309 | 19.96 | |
| 16 | $4 \times 4$ | 388649106 | 484295 | 20.26 | 1.926355433 |
| 20 | $5 \times 4$ | 304283538 | 430599 | 20.00 | |
| 24 | $6 \times 4$ | 260990624 | 461403 | 20.19 | |
| 28 | $7 \times 4$ | 218037155 | 423066 | 19.75 | |
| 32 | $8 \times 4$ | 196733139 | 415443 | 20.07 | 1.975514181 |
| 36 | $9 \times 4$ | 174894521 | 398790 | 20.19 | |
| 40 | $10 \times 4$ | 153292084 | 417555 | 19.88 | |
| 44 | $11 \times 4$ | 142358440 | 400279 | 20.23 | |
| 48 | $12 \times 4$ | 131401723 | 404199 | 20.52 | |
| 52 | $13 \times 4$ | 120450230 | 391782 | 20.17 | |
| 56 | $14 \times 4$ | 109542155 | 394545 | 20.34 | |
| 60 | $15 \times 4$ | 98877301 | 416078 | 19.75 | |
| 64 | $16 \times 4$ | 98877301 | 381393 | 20.36 | 1.989669388 |

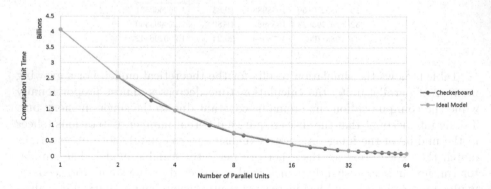

**Fig. 7.** Computation Unit Time vs Number of Parallel Units Comparison

Because the Checkerboard model features multiple Cells reading and writing to memories at the same time, the layout of the Checkerboard model reduces the communication time since the model assumes a contention-free *Off-Chip Memory*. For example, although the $2 \times 2$ layout has more PU, the $1 \times 3$ layout has one more column, so the $1 \times 3$ layout has less communication time than the $2 \times 2$ layout. The values of Table 2 are also plotted in Figs. 7 and 8 for comparison.

## 4.4    Comparison

The improvement factors in Tables 1 and 2 are listed for all cases where the PU double. The values come close to the naively expected value 2.0, but do not fully reach this perfect score due to differences in slice complexity. Table 1 shows that the theoretical model is computationally scalable. Figure 7 shows that the Checkerboard model in this graph has an almost identical curve to the theoretical model. Therefore, the Checkerboard model is also computationally scalable.

The theoretical model has a single data bus and writes the entire image after all parallel units are done working. Therefore the communication unit time remains constant for different numbers of parallel units. Figure 8 shows that the Checkerboard model (except $1 \times 1$ layout) always has less communication time than the theoretical model. Because the Checkerboard model allows multiple Core-Memory-Core communication at the same time, the Checkerboard model has better communication scalability than the theoretical model.

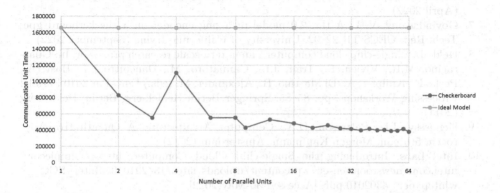

**Fig. 8.** Communication Unit Time vs Number of Parallel Units Comparison

## 5    Conclusion

In this work [19], we deliver a simulatable SystemC Checkerboard Grid of Processing Cell model and show that scalable software can be mapped onto this model. Our results show that the Checkerboard model has better communication performance and almost identical computation performance to the theoretical model, confirming that the Checkerboard GPC scales well. The Checkerboard model, while still a high-level software model, is a good starting point for a more complex and accurate SystemC model. This Checkerboard project is also proven to be a stable from other mapping projects [5,7]. The Checkerboard project also serves as a stable and flexible platform for more software simulations and enables further explorations of the true scalability of the Checkerboard GPC architecture. In future work, we aim to automate the mapping of applications to GPC platforms so that they can be programmed similar as regular shared memory architectures.

# References

1. The Tile Processor™ architecture: Embedded multicore for networking and digital multimedia. In: 2007 IEEE Hot Chips 19 Symposium (HCS), pp. 1–12 (2007). https://doi.org/10.1109/HOTCHIPS.2007.7482495
2. IEEE Standard for Standard SystemC Language Reference Manual. IEEE Std 1666–2011 (Revision of IEEE Std 1666–2005), pp. 1–638 (2012). https://doi.org/10.1109/IEEESTD.2012.6134619
3. Bohnenstiehl, B., et al.: Kilocore: A 32-nm 1000-processor computational array. IEEE J. Solid-State Circ. **52**(4), 891–902 (2017). https://doi.org/10.1109/JSSC.2016.2638459
4. Demerjian, C.: A look at the 100-core Tilera Gx. https://www.semiaccurate.com/2009/10/29/look-100-core-tilera-gx/ (10 2009), [Accessed 30-May-2022]
5. Daroui, A.: A loosely timed TLM 2.0 Model of a JEPG encoder on a Checkerboard GPC. Tech. Rep. CECS TR 22–04, University of California, Irvine (October 2022)
6. Dömer, R.: A Grid of Processing Cells (GPC) with Local Memories. Tech. Rep. Technical Report 22–01, UCI, Center for Embedded and Cyber-Physical Systems (April 2022)
7. Govindasamy, V.B.: A tlm 2.0 model of a png encoder on a checkerboard gpc. Tech. Rep. CECS TR 22–02, University of California, Irvine (September 2022)
8. Held, J.: "single-chip cloud computer", an ia tera-scale research processor. In: Guarracino, M.R., Vivien, F., Träff, J.L., Cannatoro, M., Danelutto, M., Hast, A., Perla, F., Knüpfer, A., Di Martino, B., Alexander, M. (eds.) Euro-Par 2010 Parallel Processing Workshops. pp. 85–85. Springer Berlin Heidelberg, Berlin, Heidelberg (2011)
9. Hennessy, J.L., Patterson, D.A.: Computer Architecture: A Quantitative Approach, 5th edn. Morgan Kaufmann, Amsterdam (2012)
10. Intel Labs: Introducing the Single-chip Cloud Computer. https://simplecore.intel.com/newsroom-en-eu/wp-content/uploads/sites/13/2010/05/Intel_SCC_whitepaper_4302010.pdf, [Accessed 30-May-2022]
11. von Neumann, J.: First draft of a report on the EDVAC. University of Pennsylvania (June, Tech. rep. (1945)
12. Patterson, D.A., Hennessy, J.L.: Computer Organization and Design, Revised Fourth Edition, Fourth Edition: The Hardware/Software Interface, 4th edn. Morgan Kaufmann Publishers Inc., San Francisco, CA, USA (2011)
13. Peh, L.S., Keckler, S.W., Vangal, S.: On-Chip Networks for Multicore Systems, pp. 35–71. Springer, US, Boston, MA (2009). https://doi.org/10.1007/978-1-4419-0263-4_2
14. Robert Brooks and Peter Matelski: The dynamics of 2-generator subgroups of psl(2, c). Irwin Kra (ed.) (1978)
15. Taylor, M.B., et al.: The raw processor: A composeable 32-bit fabric for embedded and general purpose computing (2001)
16. Tilera: Manycore without Boundaries: TILE64 Processor. http://www.tilera.com/products/processors/TILE64, [Accessed 30-May-2022]
17. Tilera: Manycore without Boundaries: TILEPro64 Processor. http://www.tilera.com/products/processors/TILEPRO64, [Accessed 30-May-2022]
18. Vangal, S., et al.: An 80-tile 1.28tflops network-on-chip in 65nm cmos. In: 2007 IEEE International Solid-State Circuits Conference. Digest of Technical Papers, pp. 98–589 (2007). https://doi.org/10.1109/ISSCC.2007.373606

19. Wang, Y.: A Scalable SystemC Model of a Checkerboard Grid of Processing Cells. Tech. Rep. CECS TR 22–03, University of California, Irvine (October 2022)
20. Wentzlaff, D., et al.: On-chip interconnection architecture of the tile processor. IEEE Micro **27**(5), 15–31 (2007). https://doi.org/10.1109/MM.2007.4378780

# MAFAT: Memory-Aware Fusing and Tiling of Neural Networks for Accelerated Edge Inference

Jackson Farley and Andreas Gerstlauer[✉]

Electrical and Computer Engineering, The University of Texas at Austin,
Austin, TX, USA
{jackson_farley,gerstl}@utexas.edu

**Abstract.** A rising research challenge is running costly machine learning (ML) networks locally on resource-constrained edge devices. ML networks with large convolutional layers can easily exceed available memory, increasing latency due to excessive OS swapping. Previous memory reduction techniques such as pruning and quantization reduce model accuracy and often require retraining. Alternatively, distributed methods partition the convolutions into equivalent smaller sub-computations, but the implementations introduce communication costs and require a network of devices. Distributed partitioning approaches can, however, also be used to run in a reduced memory footprint on a single device by subdividing the network into smaller operations. In this paper, we extend prior work on distributed partitioning into a memory-aware execution on a single device. Our approach extends prior fusing strategies to allow for multiple groups of convolutional layers that are fused and tiled independently. This enables trading off overhead versus data reuse in order to specifically reduces memory footprint. We propose a memory usage predictor coupled with a search algorithm to provide optimized fusing and tiling configurations for an arbitrary set of convolutional layers. When applied to the YOLOv2 object detection network, results show that our approach can run in less than half the memory, and with a speedup of up to 2.78 under severe memory constraints. Additionally, our algorithm will return a configuration with a latency that is within 6% of the best latency measured in a manual search.

**Keywords:** Machine learning · Edge Computing

## 1 Introduction

There has been a proliferation of complex machine learning (ML) problems in edge applications. Running ML applications on the edge can increase privacy, improve latency, reduce cloud communication, and require less energy [9]. However, most state-of-the-art ML networks have significant memory requirements that can exceed available memory on a resource-constrained edge device. Even

S. Henkler et al. (Eds.): IESS 2022, IFIP AICT 669, pp. 78–88, 2023.
https://doi.org/10.1007/978-3-031-34214-1_7

with virtual memory enabled, exceeding memory bounds comes with severe latency penalties due to excessive swapping between memory and disk. As a result, it is a significant challenge to run networks locally on an edge device.

Numerous commonly used neural networks contain a series of convolutional layers to process image data. Many convolutional layers, especially layers earlier in the network are feature-heavy, with a large amount of memory needed for inputs and outputs. Previous approaches to reduce memory footprints such as pruning [1,6] and quantization [5,7,11] modify the network model, require retraining, and experience accuracy degradation. Meanwhile, distributed solutions such as [8] and [12] rely on partitioning convolutions into separate tasks and running them on separate devices, but they require additional communication and a network of devices. However, such approaches can also be used to reduce the memory footprint of a computation locally on a single device.

In this paper, we extend the fused tile partitioning (FTP) approach outlined in [12] to present a memory-aware fusing and tiling (MAFAT) strategy for the execution of large feature-dominated early stages of convolutional neural networks (CNNs) on a single resource-constrained edge device. The FTP approach from [12] combines all layers into one large layer group and fuses them all together in order to reduce communication. By contrast, MAFAT creates two smaller layer groups and tiles and fuses them separately. The smaller fusings and different tilings resulting from more layer groups can reduce the maximum memory footprint of a process. We also develop a model to predict the maximum memory usage of a given MAFAT configuration. Finally, using this predictor, we propose a search algorithm that uses this predictor to return an optimized MAFAT configuration that fits within the provided memory requirement.

Results of applying our approach to a CNN used for object detection [10] show that MAFAT configurations can provide a speedup of up to 2.78 over the original model in tighter memory constraints. Furthermore, our search algorithm returns a configuration with a latency that is within 6 percent of the best measured latency for any configuration.

## 2   Motivational Example

Figure 1 depicts the latency and number of swapped bytes versus a decreasing memory constraint from running the first 16 layers YOLOv2 [10] on a Raspberry Pi3. The first 16 layers of the network are used because they are the most feature-heavy and present the greatest feature challenge to memory. Using MAFAT configurations on weight-heavy later layers will not have any added benefit and a single partition or other methods should be considered if these layers exceed memory requirements, which is out of the scope of this paper. In addition to memory for weights and input and output features, Darknet allocates scratch space in order to do a layer calculation. This scratch space can go as high as 100 MB for some layers. The largest combined memory is for layer 2. If that layer is loaded in its entirety, the processor needs at least 135 MB of memory for YOLOv2 to run cleanly.

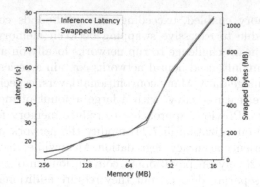

**Fig. 1.** The original YOLOv2 implementation for varying memory constraints.

Figure 1 shows a significant increase in the latency of an inference at tighter memory constraints. The CNN exceeds memory constraints at over 192 MB. Once the program goes over memory, the OS must swap data between the memory and disk. This swapping process has a demonstrated adverse affect on latency. As the memory constraints continue to shrink, the inference latency increases dramatically, with a 16 MB memory constraint over 6.5× slower than the original. This motivates a need for optimizations as presented in this paper to reduce the latency overhead due to swapping.

## 3   Related Work

The primary approaches to reduce memory on a single device are pruning and quantization. Pruning attempts to remove a portion of the model, such as weights in a filter, but this can result in asymmetric computations that can be difficult to implement [1]. Entire filters can be removed, too, such as in [6]. In both of these cases, pruning severely degrades accuracy and expensive retraining is required afterwards. Quantization of a CNN [5,7] reduces the number of bits necessary to store weights. Similarly, retraining is often needed to get better accuracy [11]. Quantization also removes model information, i.e. it also degrades the accuracy of the model. By contrast, MAFAT is able to preserve model accuracy while decreasing the memory footprint. MAFAT is orthogonal to both pruning and quantization. Because the model is preserved, MAFAT can easily be applied to a pruned or quantized network. Combinations of MAFAT and quantization or pruning have the potential to shrink the memory footprint of convolutions significantly. Some prior work has considered memory balancing and swapping overhead when scheduling multiple DNNs on edge devices [2]. By contrast, MAFAT is aimed at reducing memory swapping overhead for each individual DNN.

In addition to pruning and quantization, partitioning of models across multiple devices has been applied in distributed settings. For example, MoDNN [8] uses a one-dimensional partitioning scheme where a map-reduce algorithm can execute many of the partitions in parallel. DeepThings [12] uses Fused Tile Partitioning (FTP) to split layers into an even 2D grid and combines them via a fusing process in order for corresponding grid sections to be executed independently. Furthermore, DeepThings proposes data reuse and scheduling approaches such that adjacent partitions can use previously computed data where possible. However, all of these works are designed for computation among several devices. Because of this, communication is a primary consideration. Since MAFAT uses only a single device, alternative techniques such as partial fusing and re-tiling after a certain number of layers can result in more optimal memory usage.

## 4    Memory-Aware Fusing and Tiling (MAFAT)

This paper proposes memory-aware fusing and tiling (MAFAT) [4], which builds on the fused tile partitioning (FTP) method from [12]. FTP allows a set of convolutional layers to be split into multiple smaller sub-convolutions. Each sub-convolution consists of a tile of the original input and output feature maps, where the sub-convolutions combine and fuse corresponding tiles across all layers to execute as one unit. Instead of fusing all layers to minimize communication, MAFAT separates layers into up to two layer groups to provide additional control over memory usage. For example, if the early layers take up significantly more data than the later ones, it may make sense to tile the earlier layers more heavily. In this case, there is less memory being used in the earlier layers, but there is no significant added overhead in later layers from unnecessary tiling. Additionally, for a smaller number of fused layers, the overlap incurred will be less. This means that there is less redundant computation, and the grid of earlier layers does not have large task size disparities. In a standard $3 \times 3$ fused tiling with data reuse, the middle task does not reuse any data. Because of this, it is much larger than the surrounding tiles and its memory usage is disproportionately larger.

MAFAT currently takes any set of $n$ convolutional and maxpool layers. The layers are configured in a single layer group with all layers fused or two layer groups separated by a $cut < n$. This cut is the point at which the two layer groups are split. The first layer group will be from layer 0 to layer $cut - 1$, and the second rom layer $cut$ to layer $n$. In this way, each layer is part of one of the two layer groups. There is some additional overhead for storage of additional parameters be stored, and the cut layer must be merged in memory and re-tiled.

Potential cuts are determined in a memory-aware fashion. Collecting all the tiled data into a single input tensor and re-tiling can be memory intensive. To make this as efficient as possible, the cuts were chosen to be directly after maxpool layers. After these layers, the tensors are significantly smaller, as they have effectively just been down-sampled. In the YOLOv2 example, these potential cuts are at layers 2, 4, 8, and 12. For the two layer groups, the tiling for each group is independent of the other. This means that the first layer group could be tiled at $5 \times 5$ while the second could be tiled at $2 \times 2$. The potential tilings were all even on height and width, and were $1 \times 1$, $2 \times 2$, $3 \times 3$, $4 \times 4$, and $5 \times 5$.

---

**Algorithm 1:** Memory predictor for a single layer group

---

1  predictLayerGroup($N, M, \mathbf{W}, \mathbf{H}, \mathbf{F}, \mathbf{S}, top, bottom$)
2  $max \leftarrow 0$;
3  **for** $i \in 0..N$ **do**
4      **for** $j \in 0..M$ **do**
5          $l \leftarrow bottom$;
6          **while** $l \leq top$ **do**
7              $w_{in}, h_{in}, w_{out}, h_{out}, c_{in}, c_{out} \leftarrow \text{Grid}(l, N, M, W_l, H_l, i, j)$;
8              $scratch \leftarrow w_{out} \times h_{out} \times c_{in} \times (F_l)^2/S_l$;
9              $input \leftarrow w_{in} \times h_{in} \times c_{in}$;
10             $output \leftarrow w_{out} \times h_{out} \times c_{out}$;
11             $mem \leftarrow scratch + output + (input \times 2)$;
12             **if** $mem > Max$ **then**
13                 $Max \leftarrow mem$;
14             $l \leftarrow l - 1$;
15 return $Max + bias$;

---

## 4.1 Predicting Maximum Memory Usage

We also developed a predictor of the maximum memory usage of a given MAFAT configuration based on the maximum memory usage of the largest tile in each layer group. Layer groups generally exceed memory towards the beginning and middle of their execution. It was found that the factors that best predicted maximum memory usage were the largest combination of: (1) scratch space of tile $t$, (2) input to tile $t$, (3) output of tile $t$, and (4) output of previous layer to tile $t$. While other parameters such as the size of data reuse and size of tasks waiting in the processing queue were considered, these were found to negatively affect the ability of the predictor to accurately predict memory usage. Additionally, weights for all layers in the fusing are assumed to be in memory constantly, as well as a significant amount of additional overhead devoted to network parameters, system variables, and other data. A constant *bias* term of 31 MB was empirically determined to account for these. This bias depends on the operating system, network and hardware platform.

A memory prediction is obtained as the maximum over predicted memory usage for all tiles in all layer groups in a given cut configuration. The memory predictor for one layer group is shown in Algorithm 1. This algorithm predicts the maximum memory usage of a given layer group and tiling strategy. The inputs to Algorithm 1 are the parameters of a layer group spanning from layer *top* to layer *bottom* with an $N \times M$ tiling strategy, as well as a network configuration $\mathbf{W}, \mathbf{H}, \mathbf{F}, \mathbf{S}$ with each layer $l$ having width $W_l$ and height $H_l$, filters of size $F_l$ and a stride of $S_l$. The stride is how much the filter moves each computation. The *Grid* function in Algorithm 1 calculates and returns the dimension of a tile in layer $l$ including additional overlap following the traversal function in [12].

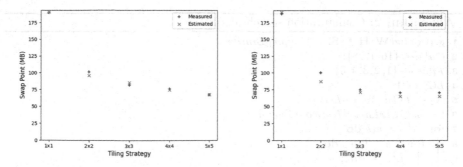

**Fig. 2.** Memory usage prediction for fully fused 16 layers (left) and for 8 fused layers with a $2 \times 2$ fused tiling on layers 9–16 (right).

Figure 2 depicts the predicted memory limit and the measured limit for a single layer group and for the MAFAT configurations with a cut at layer 8 and a $2 \times 2$ bottom tiling strategy. The measured limit was determined using the setup in Sect. 5 by decreasing the memory constraint in 1 Megabyte increments until swaps were observed. The predictor performs well in both cases.

## 4.2   Configuration Algorithm

To determine the ideal MAFAT configuration, Algorithm 2 performs a greedy search over a subset of the configuration space to find the configuration with the fewest tiles. Its goal is to return a near-optimal configuration of the network such that the end latency will be as small as possible. The inputs to the algorithm are the layer parameters and the memory limit. The relevant layer parameters are width $(W_l)$, height $(H_l)$, filter size $(F_l)$, stride $(S_l)$, and the total number of layers to be fused $(n)$. The vector of potential cuts $(Cuts)$ here is specific to YOLOv2, due to the location of the maxpool layers. A further restriction of the search space is based on a manual configuration. Specifically, no latency advantage was found for cuts at layer 4, and when there were cuts made, the best performing second layer group tiling was $2 \times 2$. The tiling strategies are also currently limited to even squares.

Algorithm 2 returns the number of tiles for the first layer group $LG_1$, the cut $cut$, and the tiling for the second layer group $LG_2$. It performs the modified search starting at the highest memory value, and slowly creates more even configurations that require more overhead, but fit in smaller memory footprints. If a configuration is found that fits in the memory limit, there is no unexplored configuration in the search space that will produce a higher memory prediction. Therefore, the latency returned should be the lowest. If virtual memory is enabled, this algorithm assumes that any additional swaps from the operating system will be slower than picking a better configuration. If no configuration can be found, then the algorithm returns the most even configuration: $5 \times 5$ into $2 \times 2$ with a cut at layer 8.

---

**Algorithm 2:** Configuration search algorithm

---

1  getConfig($\mathbf{W}, \mathbf{H}, \mathbf{F}, \mathbf{S}, n, MemoryLimit$)
2  $Cuts \leftarrow \{16, 12, 8\}$;
3  $Tiles \leftarrow \{1, 2, 3, 4, 5\}$;
4  $LG_2 \leftarrow 4$;
5  $N_2 \leftarrow LG_2$;  $M_2 \leftarrow LG_2$;
6  $l \leftarrow getMaxLayer(NetworkParams)$;
7  **for** $cut \in Cuts$ **do**
8     **for** $tile \in Tiles$ **do**
9         $LG_1 \leftarrow tile$;
10        $N_1 \leftarrow LG_1$;  $M_1 \leftarrow LG_1$;
11        **if** predictMem($N_1, M_1, N_2, M_2, \mathbf{W}, \mathbf{H}, \mathbf{F}, \mathbf{S}, cut, n$) < $MemoryLimit$ **then**
12           **return** $LG_1$, $LG_2$, $cut$;

13 **return** $LG_1, LG_2, cut$

---

## 5    Experimental Results

We applied MAFAT to the YOLOv2 object detection network. The measurements were all carried out on a Raspberry Pi3 running Raspian. The Raspberry Pi was equipped with a quad-core 1.2GHz ARM Cortex-A53 processor and a total memory size of 1 GB. During the measurements, we restricted the Raspberry Pi to a single core and a variable amount of memory from 16 MB up to 256 MB.

A separate measurement thread was created to measure system swaps in and out of memory each second. This gives information about likely places for a bottleneck. This was achieved using the vmstat command. Due to the vmstat only working at a full system level, it was crucial to keep the test environment free of as many other running processes as possible. Despite this, there is some noise in the swap measurement.

To measure memory usage of just the process, an additional thread was used that polled the process using the ps command. This way we could filter out other processes without as much added system noise. This was useful in seeing more accurately where the swapping would line up with the program.

Both of these threads however added some additional memory usage and could potentially increase swaps or create conflicts with the process. Therefore, when the latency for the process was calculated, internal measurements were used via the chrono. h library in C++ for accurate, wall clock times at a millisecond granularity. This also allowed precise measurements at the beginning and end of an inference. In this paper, the latency was measured before the input image was loaded and after the first 16 layers had executed.

To mimic a smaller edge device with minimal effort, this paper used control groups. Specifically, the cpuset and memory control groups were used to restrict the experiment to a single core and a smaller amount of memory, respectively.

This allowed for finer adjustments of memory constraints without the need for rebooting. For predictability and reproducibility, as few active processes as possible were running during final latency measurements.

## 5.1  Manual Exploration

To develop the algorithm, and to better understand the configuration performance, we first performed a manual search of different possible configurations. In the following, a MAFAT configuration with a top layer group tiling of $N_1 \times M_1$, a cut a layer $c$, and a bottom layer group tiling of $N_2 \times M_2$ is written as $N_1 \times M_1/c/N_2 \times M_2$ Using prior knowledge, the search space of possible cuts was restricted. As mentioned before, intermediate data is reduced the most by cutting the network into two layer groups at layers 4, 8, and 12, or no cut at all. In each case, all layers up to and after the cut were fused together. Additionally, the final layers were split into either $2 \times 2$ or $3 \times 3$ tiles for reducing maximum memory while still allowing for faster processing times. The tilings for the top layer group were swept from $1 \times 1$ to $5 \times 5$.

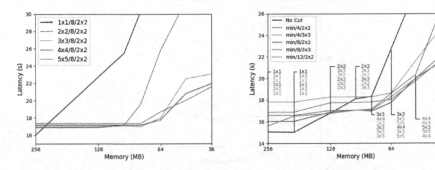

**Fig. 3.** Latency for different tilings cut at layer 8 (left) and for different cuts (right).

Figure 3 shows the effect of top and bottom layer group tiling strategies on measured latency across a shrinking memory limit. In the graph on the left, each line represents the tiling of the top layer group, which is then cut at layer 8 and fed into a $2 \times 2$ bottom layer group. Results demonstrate the superiority of finer tilings in smaller memory footprints, but also the additional overhead they generate when more memory is available. For high memory values in excess of 200 MB, the $1 \times 1$ tiling is best. On the other hand, using a $4 \times 4$ or $5 \times 5$ tiling scheme yields much better results for lower memory values.

The graph on the right shows the effect of cut placement and bottom layer group tiling strategy. The top tiling for this line is the tiling strategy (from $1 \times 1$ to $5 \times 5$) that yields the smallest latency for the given cut and bottom tiling. The best top tiling for each configuration is also annotated onto the graph at each memory point. For example, the $min/8/3 \times 3$ line represents a cut at layer 8 with the best top tiling and a $3 \times 3$ bottom tiling. It can therefore be viewed as the optimized top tiling for a given cut and bottom tiling. As seen in the graph, middle cuts at layer 8 have the fastest latency at tighter memory restrictions. It is also clear that the absence of a cut becomes costly at tighter restrictions due to additional layer overlapping. This figure also reinforces top tiling results to show that finer tilings perform better at tighter memory restrictions.

Figure 4 compares the best measured latency obtained by the MAFAT manual exploration and search algorithm to the original latencies measured from the standard Darknet implementation across decreasing memory limits. It is clear that MAFAT outperforms Darknet and reduces the latency and swaps. Interestingly, the minimum configuration for the algorithm, $5 \times 5/8/2 \times 2$, is predicted to have a maximum memory usage of 66 MB. Currently, therefore, there is not a MAFAT configuration that does not run in less than a 66 MB footprint without swapping. However, as memory restrictions get even tighter, the latency increases at a much slower rate than Darknet. This shows that the MAFAT configuration also performs much better under swapping due to more even memory usage across the execution of the network.

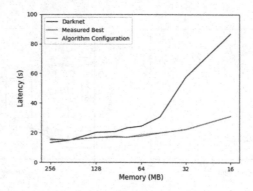

**Fig. 4.** Darknet latency compared to algorithm and minimum latency measured.

## 5.2  Algorithm Performance

Figure 4 also plots the measured performance for the configurations produced by our optimization algorithm. The differences between the algorithm and the best measured are shown to be minimal. The algorithm's specific configuration compared to the best measured can be found in Table 1. To evaluate algorithm performance, the outputs of the algorithm were calculated for the memory values in the table. This allowed for easy comparison with the existing measured data. Notably, the latency values are quite similar and are all within 6 percent of the best measured from manual exploration. Given how the algorithm relies on prior knowledge and some of the data already recorded, this level of performance is not surprising. However, the intuition behind the algorithm and the basic results should help apply it in other domains.

**Table 1.** Comparison of configurations and latencies.

| | Best Measured | | Algorithm | |
|---|---|---|---|---|
| MB | Configuration | Latency (ms) | Configuration | Latency (ms) |
| 256 | $1 \times 1$/NoCut | 15065 | $1 \times 1$/NoCut | 15065 |
| 192 | $1 \times 1$/NoCut | 15023 | $1 \times 1$/NoCut | 15023 |
| 128 | $2 \times 2/12/2 \times 2$ | 16757 | $2 \times 2$/NoCut | 16795 |
| 96 | $3 \times 3/4/2 \times 2$ | 17048 | $2 \times 2/12/2 \times 2$ | 17543 |
| 80 | $3 \times 3/8/2 \times 2$ | 16968 | $3 \times 3/8/2 \times 2$ | 16968 |
| 64 | $4 \times 4/8/2 \times 2$ | 17753 | $5 \times 5/8/2 \times 2$ | 18679 |
| 48 | $5 \times 5/8/3 \times 3$ | 19749 | $5 \times 5/8/2 \times 2$ | 19991 |
| 32 | $5 \times 5/8/2 \times 2$ | 22215 | $5 \times 5/8/2 \times 2$ | 22215 |
| 16 | $5 \times 5/8/2 \times 2$ | 31095 | $5 \times 5/8/2 \times 2$ | 31095 |

## 6    Summary and Conclusions

This paper presents memory-aware fusing and tiling (MAFAT), an expansion of existing fusing and tiling strategies in order to make feature-heavy convolutional neural network layers feasible on smaller edge devices. Originally, edge devices would have increasing latency measurements due to swapping data between the memory and disk. Many edge devices cannot spare 200 MB to run early convolutional layers, so we break up each layer into sub-convolutions that can then be grouped together and executed in a much smaller memory footprint. This paper shows that certain configurations of tiling can offer a respectable 1.37 speedup compared to the naive approach at 64 MB and up to a 2.78 speedup with only 16 MB available. Additionally, the intuition and structure behind the memory usage of the process is explored, and a simple algorithm is proposed to predict the maximum memory usage of a MAFAT configuration. Given this, an appropriate configuration can be returned for a user to use that is within 6 percent of the best measured latency from a manual exploration. The code used to take these measurements can be found at [3]. This research area can be further improved by use variable tiling, where each end tile is not the same size to allow for reduced task size variation and thus smaller footprints. We also want to generalize this algorithm to other tiling strategies and other CNNs. Currently, the end user must pre-determine what cuts make sense.

## References

1. Anwar, S., et al.: Structured pruning of deep convolutional neural networks. ACM JETC **13**(3) (2017)
2. Cox, B., et al.: Masa: Responsive multi-DNN inference on the edge. In: PerCom (2021)
3. Farley, J.: MAFAT (2021). www.github.com/JacksonFarley/MAFAT

4. Farley, J., Gerstlauer, A.: Memory-aware fusing and tiling of neural networks for accelerated edge inference. Tech. Rep. UT-CERC-21-01, UT Austin (2021)
5. Gong, Y., et al.: Compressing deep convolutional networks using vector quantization. ArXiv abs/1412.6115 (2014)
6. Li, H., et al.: Pruning filters for efficient convnets. In: ICLR (2017)
7. Lin, D.D., et al.: Fixed point quantization of deep convolutional networks. In: ICML (2016)
8. Mao, J., et al.: MoDNN: Local distributed mobile computing system for deep neural network. In: DATE (2017)
9. Park, J., et al.: Wireless network intelligence at the edge. Proc. IEEE **107**(11), 2204–2239 (2019)
10. Redmon, J., Farhadi, A.: Yolo9000: Better, faster, stronger (2016)
11. Verhoef, B., et al.: FQ-Conv: Fully quantized convolution for efficient and accurate inference. ArXiv abs/1912.09356 (2019)
12. Zhao, Z., et al.: DeepThings: distributed adaptive deep learning inference on resource-constrained IoT edge clusters. IEEE TCAD **37**(11), 2348–2359 (2018)

# Memristor-only LSTM Acceleration with Non-linear Activation Functions

Rafael Fão de Moura$^{(\boxtimes)}$, João Paulo C. de Lima, and Luigi Carro

Informatics Institute - Federal University of Rio Grande do Sul - Porto Alegre,
Porto Alegre, Brazil
{rfmoura,jpclima,carro}@inf.ufrgs.br

**Abstract.** Long Short-Term Memories (LSTMs) applied to Speech Recognition are an essential application of modern embedded devices. Computing Matrix-Vector Multiplications (MVMs) with Resistive Random Access Memory (ReRAM) crossbars has paved the way for solving the memory bottleneck issues related to LSTM processing. However, mixed-signal and fully-analog accelerators still lack in developing energy-efficient and versatile devices for the calculus of activation functions between MVM operations. This paper proposes a design methodology and circuitry that achieves both energy efficiency and versatility by introducing a programmable memristor array for computing nonlinearities. We exploit the inherent capability of ReRAM crossbars in computing MVM to perform piecewise linear interpolation (PWL) of non-linear activation functions, achieving a programmable device with a smaller cost. Experiments show that our approach outperforms state-of-the-art LSTM accelerators being 4.85x more efficient using representative speech recognition datasets.

**Keywords:** Long Short-Term Memory (LSTM) · Resistive Random Access Memory (ReRAM) · Near-sensor computing

## 1 Introduction

With the widespread usage of mobile devices and virtual assistants, the bulk of Speech Recognition applications has increased [14]. Long Short-Term Memories (LSTMs) figure as an implementation mechanism for such Machine Learning (ML) problems and have regained attention due to their capability to solve the time-dependency issues that Recurrent Neural Networks (RNNs) present. As for other Neural Network (NN) models, LSTMs are memory-intensive, having their performance bounded by the memory bandwidth available on-chip [6].

One of the solutions to suppress the memory bottleneck found on LSTM lies in bringing these applications closer to data sources. To perform such a processing in-memory computation (i.e., in-situ Matrix-Vector Multiplications (MVMs)), Resistive RAM (ReRAM) crossbars have been employed as they demonstrate higher efficiency compared to mixed-signal and digital designs [6,11,17]. Although efficiently implementing the aforementioned computation,

© IFIP International Federation for Information Processing 2023
Published by Springer Nature Switzerland AG 2023
S. Henkler et al. (Eds.): IESS 2022, IFIP AICT 669, pp. 89–100, 2023.
https://doi.org/10.1007/978-3-031-34214-1_8

ReRAM crossbars can only be used for linear computations. Moreover, the LSTMs perform on average 20 times more calls to non-linear computations (i.e., activation functions) for a single neuron compared to other NN models, such as AlexNet and Lenet, culminating in high power dissipation and energy consumption regardless of the design approach.

To bring efficiency on the execution of activation functions, several works have been proposing custom circuits, achieving high energy benefits. However, such custom logic lacks versatility, preventing reprogramming different activation functions in the same design. Also, several works have shown that depending on the input, LSTMs can exploit varied non-linear functions to improve the accuracy of their predictions [18]. In this scope, custom logic applied to LSTMs drastically reduces the possibilities of combinations of different nonlinearities.

On the other hand, Field-Programmable Arrays promise ubiquitous programmable engines to directly solve the versatility requirements of current LSTMs. Compared to custom Integrated Circuits (ICs), these configurable devices provide more flexibility and enable practical engineering for ML solutions, achieving a design cost at least 10x smaller [7]. Even though Field-Programmable Arrays bring versatility, they fall far from achieving the performance and energy efficiency levels of ICs since extra costs related to communication, routing, and IO comes out. Therefore, the trade-off between energy efficiency and versatility of LSTM designs is still an open issue to be maximized.

This work introduces a method to enable the execution of non-linear computations using ReRAM crossbars, bringing higher energy efficiency compared to Field-Programmable circuits. At the same time, this work provides a programmable-enabled activation function design that brings versatility compared to custom LSTM circuits. Given that, our main contributions are:

– We are the first to reduce the energy gap between a Field-Programmable non-linear environment and custom circuits while keeping the versatility and high accuracy provided by the Field-Programmable approach.
– We introduce the PNLU to reprogram and calculate activation functions at a smaller cost. To achieve that, we combine the inherent efficiency of ReRAM crossbars to compute MVM with Piecewise Linear interpolation (PWL).
– We compare our new LSTM design over a custom circuit (fixed activation function) and an FPAA circuit (dynamic activation functions). By using a representative speech recognition dataset, we show that our approach brings up to 2.24x computing efficiency gains over the FPAA implementation counterpart, while presenting 15% more accuracy in comparison to a custom circuit design.

The rest of this paper is organized as follows: Sect. 2 presents background on ReRAM crossbars for LSTM processing. Section 3 discusses state-of-the-art approaches to accelerate LSTMs. Section 4 introduces the proposed architecture and its details. Section 5 discusses the methodology used to evaluate this work and the results. Finally, Sect. 6 compiles future works and conclusions.

## 2   Background

### 2.1   ReRAM for In-memory NN Computing

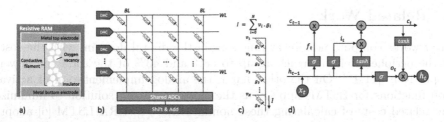

**Fig. 1.** a) Physical model of typical conductive filament-based ReRAM cell, b) Parallel dot-products implemented in a ReRAM crossbar array, c) a dot-product implemented as a sum of currents, d) LSTM cell structure

ReRAM is the most attractive Non-Volatile Memory (NVM) for NNs computing, since its cells provide many states of data representation at a low-voltage, low-latency, and dense storage [4]. Figure 1a) illustrates the physical model of a ReRAM cell. Each ReRAM cell consists of a Resistive Switching (RS) material sandwiched between two electrodes, and stores data either through the formation (set) or destruction (reset) of the conductive filament in the oxide layer by applying a programming voltage between the two electrodes [5].

The most employed representation of synapses with ReRAMs is the synaptic array. This structure is composed of a $N \times N$ ReRAM cell arrangement, which can easily implement the computation model of NNs, as illustrated in Fig. 1b). This arrangement is more efficient in chip area and power consumption and allows the design of novel accelerators that can perform MVM in the analog domain in $O(1)$ time complexity [2]. In Fig. 1c), each ReRAM cell represents a synaptic weight trough its conductance $g_i$, siting between a horizontal wordline (WL) and vertical bitline (BL). Here, $v_i$ is the input voltage signal with different amplitudes applied to each WL of the crossbar, and the output signal of each neuron is the sums-of-product of input signals with their corresponding synaptic weight. Thus, the sum-of-products is implemented as the sum of currents $I$ through each BL of the crossbar.

### 2.2   LSTM Architecture

LSTMs are modified RNN architectures that exhibit a dynamic-temporal behavior, which grants them the ability to learn order dependence in sequence-prediction problems, such as machine translation, speech recognition, and others. These networks take both the current sample $(x_t)$ and the previously calculated network state $(h_{t-1})$ as input. This feedback loop creates an internal state, which allows the network to remember and make a decision based on previous information. Figure 1d) presents a typical LSTM containing three gates (input, forget, output), block input, a memory cell, an output activation function, and peephole connections.

## 3    Related Work

Prior works compute non-linear functions in the digital domain, with the costs of the peripheral circuit reaching up to 58% and 43% of the total tile power, respectively [11,17]. On the other hand, the analog implementation of activation functions for LSTMs appears as the most prominent solution to minimize the related costs of calculating those nonlinearities [1]. ERA_LSTM [6] adopts analog approximate activation functions implemented by NNs to reduce AD conversions. However, the approach adopted on ERA_LSTM only bypasses the calculus of activation functions to another NN, which also relies on the calculus of those functions. Adam et al. [1] present a fully analog LSTM system with custom modules, such as memristor crossbars, activation functions, analog multipliers, and memory units. However, current approaches to achieve the full-analog implementation of LSTMs with ReRAMs lack either versatility or energy efficiency. Designing specialized circuits for each activation function undoubtedly achieves the best energy-efficiency but compromises the device compatibility to support custom LSTM models.

Alternatively, FPAA devices offer a promise of ubiquitous reconfigurable devices for ultra-low-power machine learning that can directly solve the enormous energy requirements of current fielded machine learning applications, as well as enable what is typically considered cloud-based machine learning in edge devices [7]. Compared to custom ICs, these configurable devices provide more flexibility and enable effective engineering cost designs for machine learning solutions. Typically the design cost for a new design is at least 10× the mask cost, requiring 10× the expected financial return to even attempt such a venture. The resulting price for designing an IC is often far too high for most engineering applications to hope to reach these financial returns. Therefore, an **optimal solution** should address the analog implementation of nonlinearities with energy efficiency and versatility.

## 4    Proposed Architecture

Figure 2a describes the overall architecture for the energy-efficient, programmable execution of LSTMs. The accelerator design is composed of tiles that are interconnected through an NoC. Each tile comprises DACs, memory buffers, a control unit, and ADCs (i.e., elements to handle the interface with other tiles and external memories). Also, an MVM Unit, a Hadamard Product Unit (HPU), and a Programmable Non-Linear Unit (PNLU) are placed inside a tile to perform the coarse grain of computations alongside the processing of an LSTM cell.

The execution flow of an LSTM described in Fig. 1 drives the data flow among the blocks inside each tile as follows: DACs convert the current input ($x_t$) and the previous hidden state ($h_{t-1}$) brought from the Local Buffers, and send them to MVM Unit. The MVM Unit computes the dot-product operations related to the four gates of the LSTM cell in parallel. The MVM results are sent to the PNLU to perform the computation of activation functions related to the four gates. The previous memory cell ($c_{t-1}$) is brought from the Local buffers, and converted to the analog domain. HPU computes the memory cell ($c_t$) output value. PNLU performs the calculus of the *tanh* over the $c_t$ value. HPU computes the hidden state value ($h_t$). Finally, both the $c_t$ and $h_t$ are converted to the digital domain and stored in the Local Buffers for the next iterations.

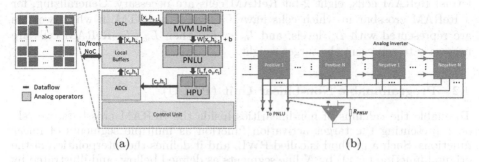

(a)                                                          (b)

**Fig. 2.** a) Overview of the proposed architecture for the energy-efficient versatile acceleration of LSTMs, b) MVM Unit in detail: organization of the ReRAM crossbar arrays.

## 4.1  MVM Unit

The implementation of the MVM Unit is presented in Fig. 2b. The MVM Unit stores the weights of the LSTM gates and efficiently computes in parallel the four dot-product operations described in Fig. 2a. Before each MVM computation, DACs take place to convert the current input data ($x_t$) and the previously-stored hidden state ($h_{t-1}$) from the memory buffer into the analog domain represented by analog voltages. Two crossbar arrays are employed to represent negative weights, containing only the weights module: one for the positive and the other for the negative weights. Then, analog inverters place at the input of the negative-weight crossbars to invert the polarity of the input voltage. Then, the MVM results are sent to the PNLU still in the analog domain to perform the computation of activation functions, depending on the requirement of the LSTM gates. To avoid drop in the signal caused by a voltage division in the connection between the MVM Unit and the PNLU, a voltage follower amp-op circuit acts by grounding the BLs and isolating neighbor layers.

The current technology of ReRAMs can deliver only cells with a limited range of conductance (typically, cells with four (2-bit) or eight (3-bit) levels). Hence, several implementations employ multiple ReRAM crossbars to compose the weight bits and combine the results by shift-and-add operations. However, such an approach may introduce two drawbacks to the proposed design: the shift-and-add operations will require unwanted AD-DA steps in the execution flow if implemented in the digital domain. Second, the shift-and-add could be implemented through the linear scaling of the voltage levels, introducing noise sources to the analog signal. Therefore, we adopt the *add method* proposed by [8] to represent the entire weight bits. In this method, several memory cells with smaller levels are added together to represent a weight with a higher number of levels. For example, to compose a 5-bit (32 levels) weight cell with 2-bit (4 levels) ReRAM cells, eight 2-bit ReRAM cells are necessary. Generalizing, for a ReRAM crossbar in which cells have $L_c$ levels, an LSTM in which weights are represented with $L_w$ levels, and $L_c < L_w$, then $L_w \div L_c$ ReRAM cells are necessary to represent the target weight.

## 4.2  Programmable Non-Linear Unit (PNLU)

To enable the calculus of non-linearities inside the ReRAM crossbars, we rely on representing the target activation function as multiple segments of linear functions. Such a method is called PWL, and it defines the interpolation of the original function ($f(x)$) by $N$ line segments as defined bellow, and illustrated by Fig. 3b.

$$f(x) \approx \begin{cases} g_1(x) = a_1 x + b1 & x_0 \leq x < x_1 \\ g_2(x) = a_2 x + b2 & x_1 \leq x < x_2 \\ g_n(x) = a_n x + bn & x_{n-1} \leq x < x_n \end{cases}$$

Figure 3a presents the circuit schematic for the PWL computation. The circuit is split into two parts: the computation of linear functions by ReRAM crossbars, and a mux to bypass the correct value of the interpolated function according to the current input value ($x$). In the ReRAM crossbar, the inputs are represented by the column-vector $[x, 1]$ and perform a MVM to generate $N$ linear functions in the format $g_i(x) = a_i x + b_i$. In this arrangement, all the $g_i(x)$ functions are computed in parallel through the sum of currents on each BL, followed by an op-amp in the voltage follower configuration. The distribution of weights in the crossbar (i.e., the $a_i$ and $b_i$ values) follows the same structure as the one presented in the MVM Unit, using the add method to compose memory cells with a higher number of bits.

After the parallel computation of the $N$ linear functions, a mux bypasses only the $g_i(x)$ output that matches the current input $x$ value. The analog circuit that generates the control signal for the mux is illustrated on the right-side of Fig. 3a. This analog circuit is composed of a series of parallel analog comparators. Each op-amp compares the input signal ($x$) to a unique reference voltage level ($V_{ref}$). $V_{ref}$ is a stable reference representing the maximum $x$ value in the domain of the interpolated function. As the analog input voltage exceeds the reference voltage

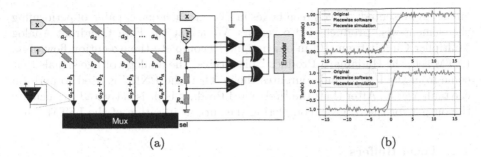

**Fig. 3.** a) The Programmable Non-linear RLU in detail: circuit schematic for the PWL computation. All programmable elements are shown in the orange color, b) Original, PWL, and simulated PWL version of *sigmoid* and *tanh* functions. (Color figure online)

at each comparator, the comparator outputs will sequentially saturate to a high state. Then, an encoder generates a signal control for the mux based on the highest-order active input, ignoring all other active inputs.

In our design, a commonplace priority encoder is not necessary to generate the control signal for the mux, as such a device introduces complexity and extra area and energy costs to the circuit. Hence, due to the nature of the parallel comparators, where each op-amp saturates high in sequence from the lowest voltage level to the highest voltage level in the voltage divisor circuit composed of the programmable resistors $R_{1:n}$, a highest-order-input selection may be realized with the employment of a set of XOR gates, followed by the usage of a simpler non-priority encoder. Last but not least, the encoder circuit itself can be made from a matrix of diodes for more simplicity.

In term of costs, to interpolate any given function with $N$ segments of lines, $(3N) - 1$ programmable resistors, $(2N) - 1$ op-amps, $N - 1$ XOR gates, and a $N : 1$ mux are needed. Such a hardware cost may look expensive in comparison with custom circuits, but this design has a much smaller cost related to any FPPA implementation. Also, since our design employs four PWL engines in the PNLU to calculate the five calls to activation functions in the LSTM flow, only $(12N) - 4$ values corresponding to the programmable resistors should be configured in contrast to thousands of elements to be configured inside an FPAA. Further discussion and comparison regarding the costs and benefits that come from the employment of the PNLU are provided in Sect. 5.

### 4.3 Hadamard Product Unit (HPU)

To calculate the Memory cell $(c_t)$ and Hidden state $(h_t)$ values for each LSTM iteration, the Hadamard or element-wise product is computed in the HPU. Since the computation flow of $c_t$ and $h_t$ contains a true dependence that hinders both from being computed in parallel, the Hadamard Unit comprises only two parallel circuits represented as two green boxes in Fig. 2a, each one capable of performing the element-wise product of two vectors. We adopt the Four-Quadrant Analog Multiplier Circuit from [10] in our design. To complete the execution flow of an LSTM cell, the Hadamard Product Unit receives the analog voltage signals that come from the PNLU and computes the $c_t$ Then the PNLU is used to perform the tanh over $c_t$. After that, the Hadamard Product Unit is activated to calculate the output for the $h_t$ gate, completing the current iteration of the LSTM cell.

### 4.4   Local Buffers

The local buffers are composed of two blocks: a memory buffer and a cache memory. Together, the memory buffers and cache comprise the memory hierarchy of a tile, which is a commonplace practice in prior ReRAM-based architectures. We employ eDRAM as the memory buffer in the proposed design and SRAM as the cache memory. Local buffers keep the input data fed to the MVM Unit, and the activation of output gates from the HPU. The cache size is set to have all the necessary input/output data of computing components mapped for one tile. By mapping the LSTM gates that share the same input onto one tile, buffer sharing can reduce the hardware overhead of local buffers.

### 4.5   Controller

The Control Unit drives the execution and data flow on each tile. This unit coordinates the data transmission between the memory buffer and cache and generates control signals for the DACs, the MVM Unit, PNLU, HPU, and ADCs. Each tile can operate in two modes: activation mode and non-activation mode. When an LSTM cell is mapped onto a single tile, it is said that this tile is operating in the activation mode. In the activation mode, the MVM products go through the PNLU and HPU. Then, the activation outputs are converted by ADCs and stored in the local buffers until the next iteration. Whenever an LSTM cell is mapped onto multiple tiles (denoted by T), T-1 tiles operate in the non-activation mode performing only MVM operations. Then, the last tile operates in the activation mode, collecting the partial sums from the corresponding T-1 tiles and proceeding with the execution flow.

## 5   Experimental Setup and Results

### 5.1   Methodology

To evaluate the proposed work, we built a simulation framework based on DNN+NeuroSim [15]. DNN+NeuroSim simulates the behavior of in-situ analog computing, such as the variability of the ReRAM, and error of ADC and DAC converters within a PyTorch wrapper, to obtain the inference accuracy. Then, the framework employs an analytical model of the ReRAM crossbar computation, including converters, memristor non-idealities, and weight mapping to compute the design's energy, area, and timing statistics. Initially, DNN+NeuroSim did not support LSTM cells or weights composed of several ReRAM cells, so we added these features and the simulation of the PNLU for the Pytorch wrapper. All activation functions were interpolated by a PWL function composed of five line segments.

**Simulation Parameters.** We use the power, area, and timing model of ReRAM crossbar arrays and the Op-Amp from [11] to design the MVM Unit and the PNLU. For the HPU, the components are extracted from related work[10]. We scale some parameters of the circuits (i.e., transistor sizes) accordingly to work with the 32 nm model. The ReRAM devices have a resistance range of $50\,k\Omega$ - $800\,k\Omega$, and the read voltage is 0.15 V. We set the sub-array size to be $128{\times}128$ for the MVM Unit and $32 \times 5$ for the PNLU. Each ReRAM cell has four bits (16 available conductance levels). Hence, 16 cells are used to represent an 8-bit weight value with the add method. The ADC and DAC models are from a fabricated ADC chip [9], and an analytical model of DACs [16]. CACTI 6.5 [13] is used to model the overhead of buffers. We limit the frequency of tiles to 10 MHz to hold the critical path of our design, which is the MVM Unit. The size of the local buffers and the number of DACs/ADCs are determined accordingly to match the throughput of the MVM Unit and the PNLU. The NN weights are quantized to 8-bit under the WAGE8 format before being mapped to the device conductance values. We use the Gaussian noise to represent the device variation for the MVM Unit and the PNLU. It has been measured that the variation is normally 0.2% for the ReRAM cells, 0.3% for the op-amps, and half LSB for the AD-DA converters [9,11,16].

**Benchmarks.** We use the bidirectional LSTM architecture [3] for the TIMIT dataset, and the LSTM model presented in [18] for the IMDb dataset as evaluation benchmarks. Regarding the employment of activation functions, the standard LSTM models for the TIMIT and IMDb datasets are built with the original *tanh* and *sigmoid* nonlinearities, refereed as the TMIT-std model and the IMDb-std model, respectively. Also, we evaluate the IMDb with the activation function comb-H-sine from [18], named IMDb-comb-H-sine model.

## 5.2 Power and Area Analysis

Figure 4 presents the power and area breakdown of a tile, and the power improvement by comparing our approach with two state-of-the-art ReRAM-based accelerators: [11], and ERA-LSTM [6]. Based on the overhead of each component, we provide a few insights into architectural details and trade-offs: **DACs and ADCs** consume a large part of the overall power and area in ReRAM-based architectures. As for ERA-LSTM, the number of DAC-ADCs is reduced due to the analog processing of the whole LSTM flow, which contributes the most to the resource-saving. **The MVM unit** in the proposed design also shows improvement over the digital and analog designs. The main reason is that the

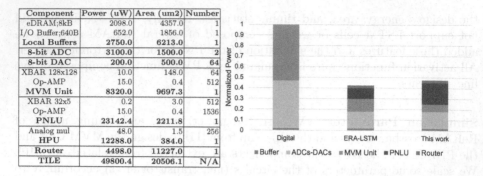

| Component | Power (uW) | Area (um2) | Number |
|---|---|---|---|
| eDRAM;8kB | 2098.0 | 4357.0 | 1 |
| I/O Buffer;640B | 652.0 | 1856.0 | 1 |
| Local Buffers | 2750.0 | 6213.0 | 1 |
| 8-bit ADC | 3100.0 | 1500.0 | 2 |
| 8-bit DAC | 200.0 | 500.0 | 64 |
| XBAR 128x128 | 10.0 | 148.0 | 64 |
| Op-AMP | 15.0 | 0.4 | 512 |
| MVM Unit | 8320.0 | 9697.3 | 1 |
| XBAR 32x5 | 0.2 | 3.0 | 512 |
| Op-AMP | 15.0 | 0.4 | 1536 |
| PNLU | 23142.4 | 2211.8 | 1 |
| Analog mul | 48.0 | 1.5 | 256 |
| HPU | 12288.0 | 384.0 | 1 |
| Router | 4498.0 | 11227.0 | 1 |
| TILE | 49800.4 | 20506.1 | N/A |

**Fig. 4.** Power and area breakdown, and power dissipation comparison with related work.

Op-Amps, the major power consumers in the MVM Unit, are shared in the proposed design. This implies the advantage of the add method, since the BL currents can be added together instead of being shifted and added after DA conversion. Using the **PNLU and the HPU** dissipates more power than its analog counterpart. However, the programmable analog computation of activation functions is necessary to achieve the best model accuracy for each dataset, as demonstrated in the next section.

### 5.3   Inference Accuracy

Table 1 presents the inference accuracy comparison. Results from [11] and ERA-LSTM are listed in the *Digital imp.* and *Analog imp.* columns, respectively. The most important result regards the accuracy levels achieved by the IMDb-comb-H-sine scenario: an increase of up to 15% compared to the IMDb-std. Here, the simple change in the activation function leads to a significant improvement in accuracy. Moreover, among all accelerator designs in this comparison, only our approach can achieve these accuracy levels, since this can reprogram itself to allow experimentation of different activation functions for LSTMs. In the *Retrained LSTM* column, we present the accuracy of our technique after retraining the LSTM models with the interpolated functions, where our design can reach the best accuracy levels. This result reveals a second level of versatility that only our work can bring to the LSTM acceleration: both LSTM and activation function model can be tuned for a given dataset with our device, achieving the best inference accuracy possible without extra hardware costs if we change any parameter of our LSTM model.

### 5.4   Computing Efficiency

Table 2 compares the computing efficiency of our design with state-of-the-art LSTM accelerators, including an FPAA-based implementation of activation functions [12] plus a ReRAM crossbar to perform MVM operations, a Digital

**Table 1.** Inference accuracy comparison

| Scenario | Inference accuracy (%) | | | | |
|---|---|---|---|---|---|
| | Baseline | Digital imp. | Analog imp. | This work | Retrained LSTM |
| TIMIT-std | 84.21 | 83.60 | 84.24 | 82.15 | 84.31 |
| IMDb-std | 76.12 | 76.01 | 75.97 | 75.92 | 76.10 |
| IMDb-comb-H-sine | 91.32 | N/A | N/A | 90.78 | 91.29 |

ReRAM-based LSTM accelerator [11], and ERA-LSTM [6]. Compared with the digital design, our approach achieves 4.85x its efficiency. ERA-LSTM is 1.27x more efficient than our design compared to the analog counterpart. This stems from the fact that ERA-LSTM employs analog custom circuits for the calculus of activation functions, which are known to be more efficient than a programmable circuit. However, our design is the only one that can achieve higher levels of accuracy due to its versatility in the choice of a programmable non-linear unit. Compared to the FPAA-based design, our approach achieves 2.24x more efficiency. Such a result can be achieved due to its simple logic inside the PNLU, which has considerable smaller costs of re-programmability than a conventional FPAA circuit. Hence, our device can deliver the versatility to model an LSTM with a smaller cost, reducing the energy gap between an FPAA dynamic activation function environment and custom circuits, while keeping the versatility and high accuracy provided by the FPAA approach.

**Table 2.** Computing efficiency comparison

| Study | ReRAM-based | Computing Efficiency (GOP/s/W) |
|---|---|---|
| Digital design | Yes | 116 |
| ERA-LSTM | Yes | 714 |
| FPAA | Yes | 250 |
| **This work** | Yes | 562 |

# 6  Conclusion and Future Work

This paper presented PNLU, a programmable ReRAM unit to accelerate nonlinearities for LSTMs in the analog domain. The proposed unit combines the inherent energy-efficient capacity of ReRAMs to perform MVM with PWL to reduce the energy gap between an FPAA dynamic activation function environment and custom circuits, while keeping the versatility and high accuracy provided by the FPAA approach. Our results show that our approach brings up to 2.24x computing efficiency gains over an FPAA implementation counterpart (dynamic activation functions), while presenting 15% more accuracy than a custom circuit design (fixed activation function). In future work, we intend to expand our approach to different NN models, and the dynamic selection of activation functions during NN inference.

# References

1. Adam, K., Smagulova, K., James, A.: Generalised analog lstms recurrent modules for neural computing. Front. Comput. Neurosci., 85 (2021)
2. Ankit, A., et al.: Panther: A programmable architecture for neural network training harnessing energy-efficient reram. IEEE Trans. Comput. (2020)
3. Evangelopoulos, G.N.: Efficient hardware mapping of long short-term memory neural networks for automatic speech recognition. Ph.D. thesis, KU Leuven Leuven, Belgium (2016)
4. Grossi, A., et al.: Experimental investigation of 4-kb rram arrays programming conditions suitable for tcam. IEEE VLSI **26**(12), 2599–2607 (2018)
5. Halawani, Y., et al.: Reram-based in-memory computing for search engine and neural network applications. IEEE JETCAS (2019)
6. Han, J., Liu, H., Wang, M., Li, Z., Zhang, Y.: Era-lSTM: An efficient reram-based architecture for long short-term memory. IEEE TPDS **31**(6), 1328–1342 (2019)
7. Hasler, J.: The potential of soc fpaas for emerging ultra-low-power machine learning. J. Low Power Electron. Appli. **12**(2), 33 (2022)
8. Ji, Y., et al.: Fpsa: A full system stack solution for reconfigurable reram-based nn accelerator architecture. In: ACM ASPLOS, pp. 733–747 (2019)
9. Kull, L., et al.: A 3.1 mw 8b 1.2 gs/s single-channel asynchronous sar adc with alternate comparators for enhanced speed in 32 nm digital soi cmos. IEEE JSSC **48**(12), 3049–3058 (2013)
10. Li, S.C.: A symmetric complementary structure for rf cmos analog squarer and four-quadrant analog multiplier. Analog Integr. Circ. Sig. Process **23**(2), 103–115 (2000)
11. Long, Y., Na, T., Mukhopadhyay, S.: Reram-based processing-in-memory architecture for recurrent neural network acceleration. IEEE VLSI (2018)
12. Moreno, D.G., Del Barrio, A.A., Botella, G., Hasler, J.: A cluster of fpaas to recognize images using neural networks. IEEE TCAS II (2021)
13. Muralimanohar, N., Balasubramonian, R., Jouppi, N.: Optimizing nuca organizations and wiring alternatives for large caches with cacti 6.0. In: 40th IEEE/ACM MICRO, pp. 3–14. IEEE (2007)
14. Park, S.H., Kim, B., Kang, C.M., Chung, C.C., Choi, J.W.: Sequence-to-sequence prediction of vehicle trajectory via lstm encoder-decoder architecture. In: 2018 IEEE IV, pp. 1672–1678. IEEE (2018)
15. Peng, X., Huang, S., Jiang, H., Lu, A., Yu, S.: Dnn+ neurosim v2. 0: An end-to-end benchmarking framework for compute-in-memory accelerators for on-chip training. IEEE TCAD **40**(11), 2306–2319 (2020)
16. Saberi, M., Lotfi, R., Mafinezhad, K., Serdijn, W.A.: Analysis of power consumption and linearity in capacitive digital-to-analog converters used in successive approximation adcs. IEEE TCAS-I **58**(8), 1736–1748 (2011)
17. Shafiee, A., et al.: Isaac: A convolutional neural network accelerator with in-situ analog arithmetic in crossbars. ACM SIGARCH **44**(3), 14–26 (2016)
18. Vijayaprabakaran, K., Sathiyamurthy, K.: Towards activation function search for long short-term model network: a differential evolution based approach. J. King Saud Univ.-Comput. Inf. Sci. (2020)

# Minimizing Memory Contention in an APNG Encoder Using a Grid of Processing Cells

Vivek Govindasamy$^{(\boxtimes)}$, Emad Arasteh, and Rainer Dömer

CECS, University of California, Irvine, USA
{vbgovind,emalekza,doemer}@uci.edu
https://www.cecs.uci.edu/

**Abstract.** Modern processors experience memory contention when the speed of their computational units exceeds the rate at which data can be accessed in memory. This phenomenon is well known as the memory bottleneck and is a great challenge in computer engineering. In order to mitigate the memory bottleneck in classic multi-core architectures, a scalable parallel computing platform called Grid of Processing Cells (GPC) has been proposed. To evaluate its effectiveness, we model the GPC using SystemC TLM-2.0, with a focus on memory contention. As an example, we parallelize an APNG encoder application and map it to the GPC and compare its performance to traditional shared memory processors. Our experimental results show improved execution times on the GPC due to a large decrease in memory contention.

**Keywords:** Memory Bottleneck · Grid of Processing Cells · SystemC TLM-2.0

## 1 Introduction

The increase in processor speeds over the past years has led to increased time spent in accessing the main memory to retrieve data. As many cores try to access the shared memory, this leads to contention and delays each core. The cores suffer from contention and their computations are halted due to sharing of the same main memory. This memory bottleneck applies to most modern CPUs which are usually shared memory processors (SMP).

To deal with slow memory access speeds, various solutions are being researched. The development of hierarchical caches is the main method to address this issue [1]. Another solution is the Berkeley RISC project, in which many complex instructions were removed because they were rarely used [2], and instead replaced with more CPU registers which are much faster to access than main memory [3,4].

In this paper, we model and evaluate SMPs and a scalable alternative called *Grid of Processing Cells (GPC)* where processors paired with local memories are

© IFIP International Federation for Information Processing 2023
Published by Springer Nature Switzerland AG 2023
S. Henkler et al. (Eds.): IESS 2022, IFIP AICT 669, pp. 101–112, 2023.
https://doi.org/10.1007/978-3-031-34214-1_9

arranged in a 2D array [5]. As a specific configuration, the GPC checkerboard architecture (Fig. 1) is aimed at addressing the memory bottleneck. The cores and memories are placed one after another, and each core has access to its own and three neighbour memories, thereby increasing data availability. The checkerboard contains several variations of a main logical component which is termed as a cell. Each cell is designed with the idea that it represents a core and components that are local to that particular core.

In this work we model the GPC architecture in SystemC TLM-2.0 [6] and map an application to it [7].

## 1.1  Problem Definition

Our main contribution in this paper is modeling and demonstrating the improvement of the GPC against the classic SMP architectures in terms of execution time and time spent in main memory access contention when running an APNG encoder on the different architectures.

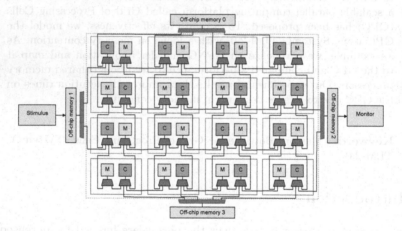

**Fig. 1.** 4-by-4 checkerboard GPC [5].

## 1.2  Background and Related Work

Over many years the general trend is that processors become faster as designers increase the clock rate but there is little increase in memory access speed [8]. This is known as the memory wall. To mitigate this problem, there has been a lot of focus on improving caches [1]. However, even the most advanced caches suffer from high miss rates if the cache size is too small or if associativity is increased too much [9]. Caches must also implement cache coherence protocols in the case of multi-core processors, and they consume significant space on the chip as well as power. Caches have given rise to Non-Uniform Memory Access (NUMA) where each core can access near memory faster than distant memory. With NUMA the time to maintain cache coherency is usually quite high [10] and leads to contention as the interconnect is shared for every core. There have been other works related to addressing the memory wall, for example the Illusion system [11], which is similar to the GPC architecture. Both have a mapping step, but in the GPC the memories surrounding each core can be accessed only by neighbours and there is no NOC to facilitate communication between distant cores. This limitation makes the GPC truly scalable because there is no NOC complexity to grow, but puts a burden on application mapping which is restricted to only local communication.

Modification to the architecture itself is one method of reducing the contention between cores. In the checkerboard GPC contention is reduced drastically as separate buses are used between the cores. Architectures similar to the GPC have been proposed in the past, such as the Epiphany-V [12]. While similarities are present, such as the fact that both use a cache-less memory model, the GPC varies in a few aspects: i) The checkerboard architecture uses a different addressing map where each memory has a different address space, ii) The GPC has no operating system running on all of the cores, and iii) GPC uses simple multiplexers-based buses instead of a complex NOC.

Our main objective in this work is to reduce memory contention through software methods, which primarily lies in the mapping operation. We also confirm that memory contention is indeed a major reason for the memory wall, and provide experimental results showing that the GPC minimizes that.

## 2   Modeling of the Checkerboard GPC

The checkerboard model [5] consists of cores with local memory which can be accessed also by their neighbours. The memory size is small and the cores themselves only perform computation on small amounts of data at a time. The small memories are referred to as on-chip memories and are expected to be as fast as caches in a multi-core computer made of static random-access memory (SRAM). The off-chip memories are larger but slower, similar to dynamic random-access memory (DRAM).

**Core Module -** The core module is the computation component of a cell (Fig. 2) and represents a complete processor core with in-order or out-of-order execution but without (or only 1<sup>st</sup>-level) cache. It contains a single socket connected to the core multiplexer. It is a SystemC module containing general arithmetic functions. The primary communication is the SystemC blocking transport interface (*b_transport*) [13] and event synchronization to prevent possible race conditions when interacting with other cores. Each core contains a main thread which performs the actual computation.

**Memory Module -** Each core has its own on-chip memory to store its data. This memory is assumed to be fast as SRAM, but small (up to 128 megabytes). The memory can only be accessed by the four neighbouring cores similar to a local scratchpad memory with explicitly managed address space. The off-chip memories on the edges of the checkerboard are larger (512 megabytes) but have slower access (DRAM).

**Core Demultiplexer Module -** In order to communicate with the neighbours, an addressing scheme for the checkerboard is required. The global address space refers to the four off-chip memories on the outside and the local address space refers to the small memories near the cores. The core demultiplexer routes addresses to the individual memories. It contains one socket to communicate with the core and four sockets to connect to the adjacent memory multiplexers. The core demultiplexer forwards *b_transport* calls from the core after performing address translation.

**Memory Multiplexer Module -** The memory multiplexer is connected to a memory and to adjacent core demultiplexers. Its purpose is to forward *b_transport* calls from neighboring cores to its memory. The memory multiplexer permits only one access at a time and performs arbitration. This allows to observe memory contention. Algorithm 1 provides the algorithm of how the time spent waiting for memory access is computed [14].

---

**Algorithm 1:** Maintaining busy state in *b_transport* inside the core multiplexer (bus access arbitration with FCFS policy)

---

initialization: busy_until = 0;
busy = busy_until - current timestamp;
**if** *busy < 0* **then**
   |   busy_until = current timestamp;
   |   busy = 0;
**end**
delay = multiplexer delay + busy;
d1 = delay;
socket->*b_transport*(transaction, delay);
d2 = delay;
memory delay = d2 - d1;
busy_until += memory delay ;

---

## 2.1   Modeling Interconnect Contention

To observe the contention in the traffic of memory transactions, we utilize timing delays in the SystemC TLM-2.0 blocking transport interface inside our interconnect. To ensure that only one transaction at a time uses each memory, the memory multiplexer stores its busy status in a state variable and delays competing transactions accordingly.

As listed in Algorithm 1, we store a timestamp marking the end of memory occupation in a variable busy_until which we initialize to zero. When a transaction arrives, we calculate the remaining time left until the memory becomes available again. If busy is negative, the transaction arrived at an idle time and busy_until is reset.

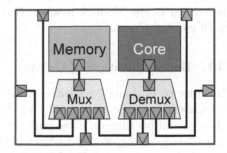

Fig. 2. Checkerboard GPC Cell.

Before forwarding the transaction to the memory (b_transport), we update the delay with the sum of the multiplexer latency and the busy delay. The transaction then processes in the memory. We observe the memory_delay by taking the time before and after the transaction and update the busy_until state variable accordingly.

In summary, our interconnect modeling accurately performs arbitration with first-come-first-serve policy and tracks the busy state of memory transactions. Aware of contention, our model enables accurate observation of any congestion in memory traffic.

## 3   Parallelized APNG Encoder Application

To test the performance of the checkerboard GPC, we need a suitable application which can be run in parallel. We choose an Animated Portable Network Graphics (APNG) encoder [15] which basically is a PNG encoder that concatenates generated PNG images with additional information such as the frame rate. PNG encoders have two main components which perform the actual image compression, the filters and the DEFLATE algorithm [16]. Filters are of five types (None, Sub, Up, Avg, Paeth) and are used to reduce pixel values. The reduced pixel values require less number of bits to transmit, providing some compression. The filtered values are sent in to the DEFLATE algorithm, which uses a combination of Lempel-Ziv-Storer-Szymanski (LZSS) and Huffman encoding to perform lossless compression. DEFLATE works better on values which are highly correlated to each other, which filtering provides [17].

Our SystemC TLM-2.0 APNG encoder consists of eight modules, namely the Color Splitter, Subtract Filter, Up Filter, Average Filter, Paeth Filter, Comparator, Compressor and APNG Encoder. The Color Splitter separates input data into individual color streams coming from the Stimulus of the encoder. The filters perform different mathematical computations which correlate pixel data, improving the compression provided by DEFLATE. The Comparator chooses the best filtered output to send to the Compressor. The Compressor uses DEFLATE to output a compressed row which is sent to the APNG Encoder module and the Monitor which writes the compressed data to a file. The APNG Encoder module generates additional information needed to create an APNG file which is written in the Monitor module. Our model performs the encoding row wise, with parallel filters.

## 3.1 Backannotation of Delays

In order to evaluate performance, we need to reflect timing in the model. We estimate the computation delay of the major APNG functions by measuring their execution time on a reference platform. Since we are mainly interested in the relative timing of major blocks in the application, we simply run the APNG encoder on a computer (2.4 GHz CPU i5-1135G7) and measure the delays with the `gprof` Linux profiler. The observed delays are listed in Table 1. We note that the filtering operations are most time-consuming in the encoder. Thus, we parallelize the filters in our model. We back-annotate the measured computation delays into the APNG SystemC model and scale them proportionally to the image size.

Every memory access by the cores results in a communication delay. In reality, not every memory access takes the same amount of time as some accesses will be to the cache and others to the main memory. However, we have not modeled caches in our SMP and single core models. Therefore, for fairness purposes we consider every memory access and multiplexer switch to be 10ns uniformly, regardless of on-chip or off-chip memory. This is still an effective measure of performance because the SMP models must perform main memory accesses frequently so that they can communicate the filtered rows to the other cores which use it, and caches are not of much use here.

**Table 1.** APNG computation delays

| Module Name | Total time | Time per frame | Time per pixel |
|---|---|---|---|
| Color Splitter | 4 s | 0.133 s | 11 ns |
| Subtract Filter | 30 s | 1.000 s | 82 ns |
| Up Filter | 33 s | 1.100 s | 88 ns |
| Average Filter | 50 s | 1.667 s | 137 ns |
| Paeth Filter | 102 s | 3.400 s | 274 ns |
| Comparator | 8 s | 0.267 s | 21 ns |
| Compressor | 14 s | 0.467 s | 38 ns |
| APNG Encoder | 1 s | 0.033s | 3 ns |

Another important metric is the contention time, which is how much time each core spends waiting for access to the main memory, as described with Algorithm 1.

## 4  Mapping APNG on the Checkerboard

To evaluate the effectiveness of the checkerboard architecture we map the APNG encoder application on it. Since not all of the memories are available to each core, it is sometimes necessary to forward data through cores. Forwarding increases the communication time for each cell. To reduce the lost time incurred by forwarding, it is better to use data by an adjacent core.

### 4.1  Checkerboard Mappings

Two checkerboard mappings have been implemented, a simpler initial mapping where individual filtering on the three colors is performed on the same core, and an improved mapping which splits the colors between cores to filter. In the initial mapping nine cores are involved in encoding with three cores forwarding data. The improved mapping has every core utilized in APNG encoding.

**Initial Checkerboard Mapping.** The main idea behind the initial mapping is to avoid the use of excessive forwarding (Fig. 3 (a)). For instance, the Subtract filter receives the red, green, and blue values from the Color Splitter. Next, it performs the computation and sends both the filtered values and the unfiltered values to the Up filter. The Up filter performs its own computation and sends the filtered Sub, Up and unfiltered values to the Paeth filter. The Paeth filter then computes the Paeth filtered output, and sends it to the Comparator while also forwarding both outputs from the Up filter and Sub filter. The same process is performed in the Average filter route. At the Comparator the least sum filtered row is chosen and sent to the Compressor. The compressed output is forwarded through neighboring cells to the right and written to the output file using the monitor. It is also sent to the APNG Encoder module for APNG encoding and forwards it to the second monitor thread.

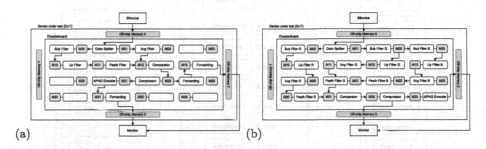

(a)                                                      (b)

**Fig. 3.** (a) An initial checkerboard mapping which attempts to minimize communication between modules. (b) An improved checkerboard mapping which splits the computational load more evenly.

**Improved Checkerboard Mapping.** While the initial mapping works, it could be further improved by splitting the filtering work of each core to three cores with each core filtering a different color component (Fig. 3 (b)). This is because some filters, such as the Paeth filter, take too much time to compute. Since there are sixteen cores available, it is possible to map every core to one module. This mapping is expected to be faster.

## 5   Experimental Results

We now compare five different SystemC models. The models are 1) Initial checkerboard (Fig. 3 (a)), 2) Improved checkerboard (Fig. 3 (b)), 3) Single core

(Fig. 4 (a)), 4) 8 core SMP (Fig. 4 (b)), and 5) 16 core SMP (Fig. 4 (c)). These models are evaluated on the basis of their execution times and amount of contention.

## 5.1   Models for Comparison

For comparison, we implement a single core and also two SMP models in SystemC. These models use a single memory with a memory multiplexer connecting the cores to the memory. The single core model performs all computations in the same core (Fig. 4 (a)). The shared memory models work similar to the checkerboard architecture, using the same communication functions to transfer pixel data between cores, but have a greater amount of contention.

The SMP with 8 cores performs the filtering operation on the different color channels in the same core (Fig. 4 (b)). Doubling the number of cores provides a 16 core model in which the cores perform less work but communication is increased per unit time leading to higher contention (Fig. 4 (c)).

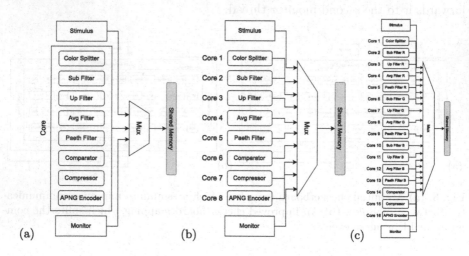

**Fig. 4.** Models for comparison, (a) single core architecture, (b) 8 core SMP where threads run in parallel, (c) 16 core SMP with shared memory.

## 5.2   Measurement of Delays

To measure delays, we create global variables of type *sc_time* called *Computation_Time*, *Read_Time*, *Write_Time* and *Contention_Time*. These variables provide an accurate value of how the time in each SystemC model is spent, and are present in every model. The *Computation_Time* (*Comp_Time*) is the summation of time spent by every core on the times listed in Table 1.

*Read_Time* and *Write_Time* keep track of the total time spent by the model accessing the memory. Added together they reflect the *Memory_Access_Time* or the *MA_Time*.

Lastly, the *Contention_Time* (*Cont_Time*) is the total time spent by every core waiting to access the memory. This time can easily exceed the execution time of the model if there are a lot of cores attempting to access the memory at the same time, as each core will be waiting to access the memory and all of these times add up to the *Contention_Time*.

## 5.3    Simulated Time Results

With the three types of delays back-annotated, we obtain measurements on the five SystemC models. Table 2 shows the variation in model timings as the clock rate is gradually increased, thereby decreasing computation time per module and increasing the frequency of memory access requests. The five SystemC models

**Table 2.** Table for simulated timing results

| Model Name | Exec Time (Speedup) | Comp Time | MA Time | Cont Time |
|---|---|---|---|---|
| **Clock rate of 0.25 GHz** | | | | |
| Single Core | 714.617 s (1x) | 707.231 s | 4.619 s | 6.791 s |
| SMP with 8 Cores | 326.703 s (1x) | | 18.518 s | 27.130 s |
| SMP with 16 Cores | 131.946 s (1x) | | 18.525 s | 29.992 s |
| Initial Checkerboard | 334.866 s (1x) | | 27.291 s | 1.388 s |
| Improved Checkerboard | 122.943 s (1x) | | 28.296 s | 1.130 s |
| **Clock rate of 0.5 GHz** | | | | |
| Single Core | 361.818 s (1.98x) | 353.615 s | 4.619 s | 6.791 s |
| SMP with 8 Cores | 166.704 s (1.96x) | | 18.518 s | 61.124 s |
| SMP with 16 Cores | 81.454 s (1.62x) | | 18.525 s | 64.398 s |
| Initial Checkerboard | 174.859 s (1.92x) | | 27.291 s | 0.699 s |
| Improved Checkerboard | 70.008 s (1.76x) | | 28.296 s | 2.676 s |
| **Clock rate of 1 GHz** | | | | |
| Single Core | 185.419 s (1.96x) | 176.808 s | 4.619 s | 6.791 s |
| SMP with 8 Cores | 86.703 s (1.92x) | | 18.518 s | 78.675 s |
| SMP with 16 Cores | 59.332 s (1.38x) | | 18.525 s | 93.821 s |
| Initial Checkerboard | 94.855 s (1.84x) | | 27.291 s | 0.354 s |
| Improved Checkerboard | 43.336 s (1.63x) | | 28.296 s | 2.564 s |
| **Clock rate of 2 GHz** | | | | |
| Single Core | 97.219 s (1.91x) | 88.404 s | 4.619 s | 6.791 s |
| sMP with 8 Cores | 48.423 s (1.81x) | | 18.518 s | 88.403 s |
| SMP with 16 Cores | 45.426 s (1.31x) | | 18.525 s | 101.670 s |
| Initial Checkerboard | 54.853 s (1.73x) | | 27.291 s | 0.182 s |
| Improved Checkerboard | 30.001 s (1.43x) | | 28.296 s | 2.712 s |
| **Clock rate of 4 GHz** | | | | |
| Single Core | 53.119 s (1.83x) | 44.202 s | 4.619 s | 6.791 s |
| SMP with 8 Cores | 38.048 s (1.26x) | | 18.518 s | 90.867 s |
| SMP with 16 Cores | 30.677 s (1.13x) | | 18.525 s | 116.412 s |
| Initial Checkerboard | 34.852 (1.57x) | | 27.291 s | 0.096 s |
| Improved Checkerboard | 23.332 (1.31x) | | 28.296 s | 2.785 s |
| **Clock rate of 8 GHz** | | | | |
| Single Core | 31.069 s (1.71x) | 22.101 s | 4.619 s | 6.791 s |
| SMP with 8 Cores | 38.047 s (1.00x) | | 18.518 s | 91.792 s |
| SMP with 16 Cores | 38.308 s (1.03x) | | 18.528 s | 119.683 s |
| Initial Checkerboard | 24.852 s (1.41x) | | 27.291s | 0.053 s |
| Improved Checkerboard | 19.999 s (1.17x) | | 28.296 s | 2.619 s |

are compared at different assumed processor clock rates. The clock rates have been chosen to start at 0.25 GHz and are doubled up to 8 GHz in our simulation.

An important assumption made intentionally is that no cache memory exists in any model. The reasoning for this is that we want to observe memory contention directly, undisturbed by caching behaviour. In other words, for a fair comparison we model all memories as fast and thus do not need caches.

Table 2 shows the comparison of the three types of delays and the overall execution time. Time spent in computation linearly reduces, but has limited effect on the total execution time as the contention time goes up in every model, to varying degrees. The increase in contention time is the reason why execution times start to show less improvement.

Plotting the values from Table 2 provides insight on the change in execution time as the clock rate is doubled (Fig. 5). For the single core model, it is seen that the decrease in computation speed leads to great increase in speedup, until a certain point where diminishing returns are observed. The shared memory processors start off with low execution time, but they start to stagnate at around 4 GHz.

The *Memory_Access_Time* or *MA_Time* varies for each of these models even though the amount of pixels they process is the same. This is because simpler models, like the single core model, need to access the memory only two times (from the stimulus and to the monitor) when processing a row of pixel data. Other models, like the checkerboard, need to pass on the data between adjacent cores, which involves a lot more reading and writing from and to memories. The SMP models need to access the main memory frequently, as almost every core needs to access new data to continue data processing.

## 5.4    Observations and Comparison

The initial checkerboard mapping starts with an execution time similar to the 8 core SMP model, but quickly accelerates as the clock rate is increased. The improved checkerboard is as fast as the 16 core SMP at low clock rates, but is twice as fast when the clock rate reaches 8 GHz. At low clock rates, the limiting factor is the number of cores, and not the memory access contention, whereas at higher clock rates this trend is reversed.

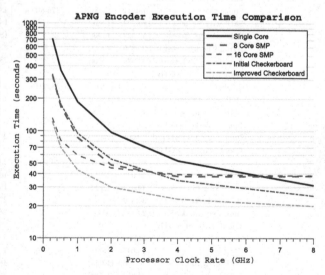

**Fig. 5.** APNG Encoder execution time scaling. Note that the graph y axis is in log scale.

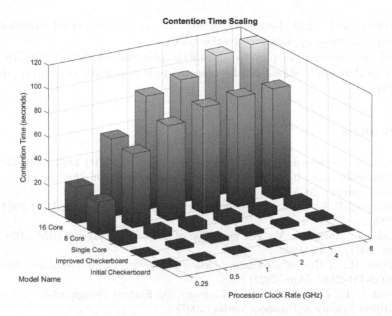

**Fig. 6.** Contention time scaling with increase in clock rate for the five SystemC models.

Figure 6 shows the increase in contention as the clock rate increases. This increases the rate at which memory is accessed by the cores so that they can process more data, which leads to a rise in contention time. For the single core model minimal contention exists because the cores are accessing the memory along with the stimulus and monitor. The initial checkerboard mapping has a linear decrease in contention, but the improved checkerboard suffers from a slight increase. The reasoning for the reduction in contention for the initial mapping is that when the clock rate increases the shorter memory accesses appear to come first, and this leads to a decrease in contention as shortest job first (SJF) reduces wait time. This does not seem to be the case for the SMP models however, as they have a noticeable increase in contention as the clock rate increases and the execution time starts to stagnate. Therefore the checkerboard architecture is a good alternative to shared memory processors as clock rate increases, its contention is much less.

# 6   Conclusion

The increase in processor speeds over the years has resulted in much faster computers but this trend has been hampered due to slower memory speed increases. The newly proposed checkerboard architecture is one possible way to mitigate the effects of slower memory access speeds, as shown by our experimental results.

In future work, we aim to provide more accurate comparisons by also including caches for our SMP models. Further, we would like to continue our modeling by lowering the level of abstraction of our cores to instruction set simulators [18] and mapping more applications to the GPC.

In the longer term, we plan to address the programmability of the GPC architecture so that applications can be mapped to it automatically by an advanced compiler.

# References

1. Smith, A.J.: Cache memories. ACM Comput. Surv. (CSUR) **14**(3), 473–530 (1982)
2. Tanenbaum, A.S.: Implications of structured programming for machine architecture. Commun. ACM **21**(3), 237–246 (1978)
3. Patterson, D.A.: Reduced instruction set computers. Commun. ACM **28**(1), 8–21 (1985)
4. Cocke, J., Markstein, V.: The evolution of RISC technology at IBM. IBM J. Res. Dev. **34**(1), 4–11 (1990)
5. Dömer, R.: A Grid of Processing Cells (GPC) with Local Memories, Tech. Rep. CECS-TR-22-01 (Apr. 2022)
6. Grötker, T., Liao, S., Martin, G., Swan, S.: System Design with SystemCTM. Springer Science & Business Media (2007)
7. Govindasamy, V.: Mapping of an APNG Encoder to the Grid of Processing Cells Architecture, Tech. Rep. CECS-TR-22-02 (2022)
8. McKee, S.A.: Reflections on the memory wall. In: Proceedings of the 1st conference on Computing frontiers, p. 162 (2004)
9. Patterson, D.A., Hennessy, J.L.: Computer organization and design ARM edition: the hardware software interface. Morgan kaufmann (2016)
10. Blagodurov, S., Zhuravlev, S., Dashti, M., Fedorova, A.: A Case for NUMA-aware Contention Management on Multicore Systems. In: 2011 USENIX Annual Technical Conference (USENIX ATC 2011) (2011)
11. Radway, R.M.: Illusion of large on-chip memory by networked computing chips for neural network inference. Nat. Electron. **4**(1), 71–80 (2021)
12. Olofsson, A.: Epiphany-v: A 1024 processor 64-bit risc system-on-chip, arXiv preprint arXiv:1610.01832 (2016)
13. IEEE Standard for Standard SystemC Language Reference Manual, IEEE Std 1666–2011 (Revision of IEEE Std 1666–2005), pp. 1–638 (2012)
14. Arasteh, E.M., Dömer, R.: Improving parallelism in system level models by assessing PDES performance. In: Forum on specification & Design Languages (FDL), vol. 2021, pp. 01–07. IEEE (2021)
15. Parmenter, S., Vukićević,V., Smith, A.: APNG Specification by Mozilla. www.wiki.mozilla.org/APNG_Specification. (Accessed 12 Aug 2021)
16. Deutsch, P., Gailly, J.-L.: Zlib compressed data format specification version 3.3,' RFC,: May, p. 1996. Tech, Rep (1950)
17. Sayood, K.: Chapter 9. Lossless compression handbook. Elsevier (2002)
18. Herdt, V., Große, D., Le, H.M., Drechsler, R.: Extensible and configurable RISC-V based virtual prototype. In: Forum on Specification & Design Languages (FDL), vol. 2018, pp. 5–16. IEEE (2018)

# Engineering Applications of Artificial Intelligence Targeting Embedded Systems

# Analysing the Characteristics of Neural Networks for the Recognition of Sugar Beets

Luca Brodo[✉], Stefan Henkler[✉], and Kristian Rother[✉]

Hamm-Lippstadt University of Applied Sciences, 59557 Lippstadt, Germany
luca.brodo001@stud.fh-dortmund.de,
{stefan.henkler,kristian.rother}@hshl.de

**Abstract.** Neural Networks (NNs) are used in various application areas to identify objects. Reliable behavior of NNs is an important aspect, especially for embedded systems. In this paper, we focus on the analysis of NNs to find correlations between their characteristics in order to be reliable and predictable in time, with the aim of making sugar beet recognition more transparent. Although obtaining promising results, as we are only going to focus on analysing models and finding correlations between some of their characteristics, this paper is only the first milestone towards using this correlation to optimize smart farming applications to improve the production and sustainability of the plantations around the world.

**Keywords:** Neural Networks · Embedded Systems · Smart Farming

## 1 Introduction

In the last years there has been an increased focus on integrating cutting-edge technology with precision farming to improve quality and quantity of agricultural production, while at the same time lowering the inputs - like manual labour - significantly [14]. This system is also known as "smart farming" and it is based on the adoption of autonomous robots, which could be both wheeled robots and Unmanned Aerial Vehicles (UAVs), and it has been enabled by the astonishing advancements in the field of the Internet of Things (IoT).

Smart Farming allows more cost-efficient and timely production and management practices, as showed by Glaroudis et al. in [9], and at the same time, the reduction of the inherent climate impact by enabling real-time reactions to infestations, such as weed, pest or diseases, and by enabling a more adequate use of resources such as water, pesticides or agro-chemicals [14].

This research is supported by a grant from the Ministry of Economic Affairs, Industry, Climate Action and Energy of the State of North Rhine-Westphalia (MWIDE) as part of the 5G-Landwirtschaft-ML project in the context of the program 5G.NRW (01.05.2022 - 31.12.2024, grant number 005-2108-0039).

One of the cultivations which will benefit immensely by the adoption of smart farming is the sugar beet. The *Beta vulgaris L*, commonly referred to as sugar beet, is ranked as the second most cultivated sugar crop all over the world next to sugarcane [2]. As showed by May in [21], being a slow-growing crop early in the season, this plant seems to be a very poor competitor against weed, a claim also backed up by Schweizer in [29], which reports that sugar beet root yields can be reduced by 26-100% by uncontrolled weed growth.

As herbicides are still the most used method to control weed infestations ([4]), in order to limit their use and therefore the impact they have on the environment, the new frontier for weed management is to automatize the more traditional mechanical techniques ([6,19,25]). Mechanical techniques, and even techniques which use selective spraying of herbicides, however, require the sugar beet to be localized before they can be applied to avoid ruining the plantation.

Although examples of different techniques employed for the recognition tasks are not uncommon ([16,33]), these type of tasks are usually carried on by Convolutional Neural Networks (CNNs) ([7,22,23,26,30]).

CNNs, however, impose great challenges to the developers due to their unpredictability. For example, in real time applications, classification time is of the highest importance since it affects the ability to respect deadlines. Furthermore, the performance of CNNs is influenced by a multitude of factors and, being able to predict their performances before their deployment, will allow engineers to precisely model the application to tailor them for the network of their choice.

In challenges such as the ImageNet classification challenge ([28]) the ultimate goal is to achieve the highest accuracy possible, neglecting other performance metrics like inference time [3].

Although accuracy is of high importance, in practical applications other metrics are to be considered as well, depending on the different requirements. As pointed out by *Canziani et al.* in [3], metrics like inference time, parameters and operations count are hard constraints for the deployment of Neural Networks in practical applications. Furthermore, training time is often a time consuming process which highly depends on factors like the complexity of the task, size of the network and training set ([24]).

Finding relations between these characteristics and other factors as well, like influence of a given input feature to the prediction of the model ([11]), will allow us to optimise applications, saving time and resources in the process. In this paper, we are going to investigate whether it is possible to make those predictions by empirically studying the metrics which can influence CNNs' performances and find correlations amongst them in order to be able to be predictable, especially time-wise. In other words, the approach presented attempt to compare and evaluate the performance of CNNs under different conditions and workloads. In comparison, we look at the characteristics of CNNs in order to develop techniques to measure performance and from this to determine - i.e. predict - the behavior of CNNs.

As a result of our investigation, we aim to develop a toolbox for the employment of CNNs in sugar beet recognition. In the next section we give an overview of the related work. In Sect. 3, we introduce the benchmarking tool utilized. The analysis of the NNs characteristics including the benchmarking results are presented in Sect. 4. We conclude our paper with a summary and outlook in Sect. 5.

## 2   Related Work

Regarding the study of neural networks' performances, both academic and industrial organizations have already developed numerous benchmark solutions to evaluate the behaviour of neural networks under different workloads and on different devices. For example, authors of [18] and [13] have proposed benchmarks of neural networks specifically for mobile devices. *Hendrycks et al.* in [10] developed a benchmark to assess the robustness of image classifiers under condition of perturbations.

*Reddi et al.* in [27] propose a benchmark, namely MLPerf, to evaluate inference of Machine Learning system under various workloads. They divided workloads under high level tasks, such as image classification, and they provide a reference model for it.

*Zou et al.* in [34], among other contributions, proposed a benchmark suite to analyse neural networks' training time of eight different state-of-the-art models under six different application domains. The metrics collected during the profiling are throughput, i.e. the amount of input samples processed by the networks, GPU utilization, FP32 utilization, i.e. the percentage of floating operations done during training, since typically training CPU utilization and Memory Consumption.

A similar goal described in the previous section is also the one shared by Unterthiner et al. in [31], which demonstrates that the prediction of accuracy of neural networks using the weights is viable. More generally, in recent years, other authors have shown possible predict the performance of neural networks by parameters ([5,20]). In this paper, however, rather than on the parameters, we will rely upon methods to find those characteristics empirically, i.e. through benchmarking.

## 3   Analysing the Models

As mentioned previously, we are going to predict neural network characteristics based on an empirical analysis carried on through benchmarking. Benchmarking is a widely used method to evaluate the performance of a system, either software or hardware, whose main goal is to produce consistent and precise measurements of said systems ([1]). High precision and reliability in benchmarks could bring knowledge about the timing behaviour of tasks, more specifically their worst-case execution times (WCETs), which is of the highest importance for building reliable and dependable real-time systems ([32])

According to *von Kistowski et al.* in [15], benchmarks should follow five key characteristics in order to be reliable, namely relevance, reproducibility, fairness, verifiability and usability. Relevance measures how close the behavior of the benchmark relates to the behaviors it is trying to test. Reproducibility is the ability to consistently obtain similar, if not equivalent, results if the benchmark is tested on the same environment ([15]). "Furthermore, a benchmark has to be fair, namely it has to allow the results obtained in different systems with completely different hardware and software to be comparable. A good benchmark should be also able to provide trustworthy results and also results whose trustworthiness can be verified. To ensure the verifiability of these results, good benchmarks usually run self-verification tasks during run-time, for e.g. if hyper-threading is still active when it should not. Finally, usability is the characteristics of a benchmark which aims to remove roadblocks for users to run the benchmark in their environments.

Some of these characteristics are tightly correlated to one another, for e.g. reproducibility is highly related to the ability of describing the environment in perfect detail, so that it could be performed on the same environment and expect similar results, which is also an important factor for usability. In general, however, it is important to have a benchmark tool which respects those characteristics. Such tool will allow us to study the behaviour of neural networks in order to find correlations amongst the characteristics of neural networks, therefore the main requirement it needs to adhere to is flexibility. Applications in the field of sugar beet recognition may be subject to various requirements and different conditions, hence the tool must be able to reflect that. In other words, it should be flexible enough so that we are able to configure it in multiple ways to reflect the various condition, but at the same time it must also be able to produce results that are specific for our scope, i.e. finding the correlation between different metrics. Furthermore, we need the results to be verifiable and trustworthy. Being the foundation for further steps, the results need to be trustworthy and they need to be precise and accurate enough, so that they can be reasoned about.

For the porpuse of this paper, the choice of the architecture is limited amongst Resnet, Alexnet and VGG. Both the indication regarding the dataset and the choice of the models will be indicated in an external configuration file by the user. The tool will read this file before initializing the test, in order to collect the necessary information needed to run properly. This configuration file helps to improve both flexibility and usability, in addition to automatically creating a documentation of the run for reproducibility.

The actual implementation of the tool is done using Python and revolves around the *fastai* library. This library is built on top of Pytorch, a very common library for machine learning, and offers powerful functions and high flexibility without a significant drop in performance. [12]

*Fastai* perfectly suits the goals of the benchmarking tool as it is *"approachable and rapidly productive, while also being deeply hackable and configurable"*. [12]

# 4    Analysis of the Characteristics

Thanks to the knowledge and the tool described in the previous section in our hands, we can now move on to discuss a real-world use case as a proof of concept. For the purpose of this paper, the characteristics we are mainly focusing on are inference time, accuracy, training time and loss. The experiment has been run on the same machine running Ubuntu 20.04.3 LTS (Focal Fossa). For the specific of the machine, please refer to Table 1.

**Table 1.** Specifics of the machine which run the experiments

| CPU | 2x AMD EPYC 7452 32-Core Processor |
|---|---|
| CPU MHz | 1499.324 |
| CPU max MHz | 2350,0000 |
| CPU min MHz | 1500,0000 |
| Total memory | 1 TB (16 × 64 GB) |
| GPU | Nvidia A100-PCIE-40 GB |
| Number of GPUs | 7 |

The models have been trained on the GPUs, using the default configuration offered by *Fastai*. Furthermore, the models have not been pre-trained, hence no transferred learning is applied, and the models have been trained using full precision. Although a relatively powerful machine, and rather different from the mobile-robots used in the solutions we discussed, this experiment gives us important insights to how such analysis can be carried on.

We are going to use the dataset proposed by *Giselsson et al.* in [8], which we are going to refer to as the 'plant_seedlings_v2' dataset. This dataset contains ~1000 RGB images with a pixel density of 10 pixels per mm divided in 12 different plant species. Even though the dataset is mainly focused on seedlings and it contains pictures of other plants as well, this will give us proper insights of the models' behaviours in a farming setting.

The first metrics we are going to analyse are training time, number of epochs and accuracy. We will study those metrics in order to recognize some patterns and use those to be able to find correlations between the three, with the final aim being able to predict one of them, whilst knowing the others. We are going to start our analysis by studying the results obtained when the models are trained for 100 epochs, which are shown in Fig. 1a and 1b.

Alexnet is the model that achieved the lowest accuracy, overall reaching ~86% after 99 epochs. The highest accuracy has been achieved by Resnet101, peaking at ~97% after 66 epochs. Moreover, VGG16 and VGG19 achieved the same peak accuracy at ~95%, however VGG16 required 13 epochs less (43 compared to the 56 needed for VGG19). Similarly, Resnet18 and Resnet34 achieved comparable top accuracies at 94.39% and 94.48% respectively, however Resnet34 required considerably less time to reach this number peaking after 62 epochs, while Resnet18 achieved this number when the training cycle was almost done, namely after 96 epochs.

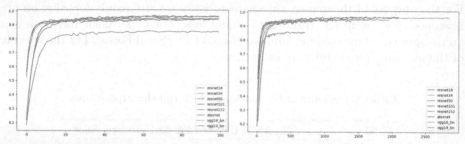

(a) Accuracy achieved by the models after being trained for 100 epochs. The x axis is the number of epochs, while the y axis is the accuracy achieved

(b) Accuracy achieved when training for 100 epochs in relation with training time. The x axis is the training time in seconds, while the y axis is the accuracy achieved

**Fig. 1.** Training results of all models calculated over 100 epochs. The accuracy is calculated over the training set.

Figure 1a shows the response of all models during the training based on the epoch used for training. The response of the model shows that, within the first ten epochs, the accuracy increases quickly and tends to stabilise afterwards, increasing slowly over time. However, we can observe a compact graph, meaning all the models (besides Alexnet) achieved accuracies not too far off from each other. As a matter of fact, the difference in accuracy between the highest performing model (Resnet101) and the lowest performing model (Resnet18) was only 3%.

Figure 1b, on the other hand, depicts the accuracy graphed over training time. Alexnet took the least amount of time to finish the training cycle (747 s), however Resnet18 took only ~40 s more and reached a far better accuracy(94% compared to 85%). Resnet152 took 47 min and 30 s (2851 s ) to complete the test and is the model that required the most time.

In Fig. 2, we can analyse the loss calculated for the models during the training. Figure 2a refers to the loss calculated over the training set, while Fig. 2b depicts the loss calculated over the validation set, which comprises of pictures not included in the training set. As shown in Fig. 2a, all the models (besides Alexnet) reached closed to zero training loss within the first 30 epochs. Usually, when the training loss is close to zero, we are expecting a case of over-fitting, which would be proven by a high validation loss. We can then study the validation loss of the models in Fig. 2b. From their response, we can observe that the validation loss does not increase drastically. On the contrary, the difference between validation loss and training loss is rarely more than 0.4. Furthermore, the curve seems to be quite stable, especially for shallower networks, and the validation loss tends to increase slowly.

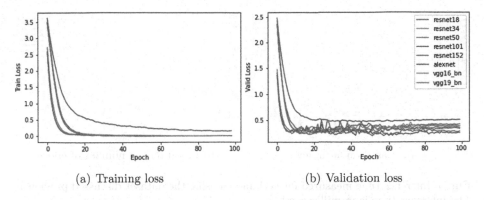

(a) Training loss                    (b) Validation loss

**Fig. 2.** Training loss and validation loss of all models calculated over 100 epochs

As we are mostly focused on sugar beet recognition, it is safe to assume use cases where field robots would scan the field to recognize the vegetation, similarly to the one proposed by *Lottes et al.* in [17]. In such setting, the time taken to classify the image, ultimately, results in a soft deadline, as the time taken to scan the field is greatly influenced by it, therefore being able to estimate the needed inference time could help optimise this part of the application.

In order to test for inference time, we are going to use a dataset composed of ~120 pictures taken from the original dataset. These pictures were taken before starting the process, therefore they have not been used for training. The results are shown in Fig. 3.

Figure 3a shows the inference time based on the accuracy, while Fig. 3b shows the inference time based on the epoch used to train.

From Fig. 3a we can start to observe some rather interesting properties. For each model, as they achieve accuracy less than 88%, the inference time is rarely measured to be more than 60 ms, with only 2 exceptions (~100 ms and ~390 ms). Furthermore, the only model that achieved an accuracy smaller than ~82% is Alexnet.

For accuracies over 88%, although the behaviour of the models seems to be less compact, the inference time rarely measures more than 100 ms, with only two outliers(~135 ms and ~180 s).

From Fig. 3b we can see that, with the exception of the outliers we identified before, the number of epochs that measured the highest value for inference is 30. As a matter of fact, when trained for different numbers of epochs, the models never require more than 100 milliseconds to process the images.

A closer investigation of the individual performance of each model shows further interesting aspects. For the purpose of this experiment, we are going to analyse only Resnet101 and Resnet152, whose behaviour is shown in Fig. 4a and Fig. 4b respectively. For both models, we can see that the highest accuracy is achieved when trained for only one (~91% for both) and two epochs (slightly lower of 91% for Resnet18 and ~90% for Resnet152). For the other epoch, the accuracy achieved was consistently lower than 90%. In the case of Resnet101 it

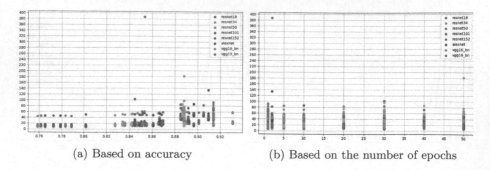

(a) Based on accuracy                    (b) Based on the number of epochs

**Fig. 3.** Inference time measured for each model using the dataset discussed previously. The inference time is in milliseconds

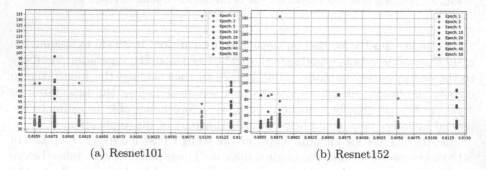

(a) Resnet101                            (b) Resnet152

**Fig. 4.** Inference time measured for Resnet101 and Resnet152. The inference time is in milliseconds.

resulted in an overall faster behavior when trained for ten and five epochs, with an inference time of less than 45 ms, with the exception of only two occasions. Although the fastest, the model trained with these epochs also achieved the lowest accuracy. The slowest inference time has been achieved when the model has been trained for two epochs, with an inference as high as 135 ms. However, the model achieved the worst overall performance when trained for 30 epochs. As a matter of fact, even though it measured the lowest inference time when trained for two epochs, this occurred in only one case, while, when trained for 30 epochs, for a considerable amount of pictures, the inference time was in a range between 57 and 95 ms. Resnet152, on the other hand, showed more consistent results, with an inference time being in the range of 40 to 90 ms for all epochs with the exception of one case where it reached 180 ms. The fastest inference time for this model is measured when the model has been trained for 20 epochs.

From this investigation we can conclude that the performances of these two models are quite comparable, when it comes to inference. Both in terms of inference time and accuracy achieved, the two models show similar results, albeit for different levels of training. For example, in the case of Resnet152, with a training time of 580 s (20 epochs), we obtain a model that can make predictions in a range between 45 and 85 ms with an accuracy of ~89%. In the case of Resnet101, we can obtain similar results (prediction time between 70 and 30 ms with an accuracy of ~89%) with a training time of 210 s (10 epochs).

We can also run the tool to discover which pictures took the most amount of time to be processed. Figure 5 shows the ten slowest images for each model graphed based on their sizes.

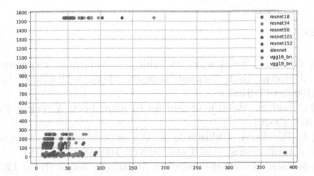

**Fig. 5.** This graph shows the size in kb (y axis) of the ten slowest images over the time taken to be processed (x axis)

The graph shows a rather compact and stable behaviour, with the slowest time measured for images having a size bigger than 1500 kb.

For pictures of more than 100 kb and less than 300 kb, the inference time is between 0 and 100 ms, with each model performing rather similarly.

For this experiment, both for training and for testing inference, we used a dataset with images having rather similar size and resolution, therefore this analysis is not as valuable as expected.

## 5   Summary and Outlook

Sugar beet plantations, due to their poor performances against other competitors like weed, will benefit from the advancements brought by the introduction of smart farming techniques. Most of the solutions in this field proposed methodologies for increasing production and sustainability based on the recognition and localization of sugar beets using Neural Networks. Neural Networks, however, impose obstacles which, despite their great flexibility, make tailoring applications around them challenging.

In this paper, we investigated how the analysis of the characteristics of Neural Networks brings to find correlations between them that can be used to predict the performances of the networks in a time-wise reliable way. The output of our investigation was a software tool which we used to study a use case to demonstrate how we can effectively find these correlations and these characteristics, mentioning how they could be used in future applications.

Even though we achieved promising and insightful results, this paper leaves many interrogatives open which need to be explored in future works. First of all, we only investigated some of the characteristics which neural networks possess and can be correlated with each other. For example, we did not focus on parameters which influence the performances of the networks, like for e.g. learning rate, batch size or throughput. It is left for further studies to identify other characteristics that can be worth studying to find more correlations.

# References

1. Beyer, D., Löwe, S., Wendler, P.: Reliable benchmarking: requirements and solutions. Int. J. Softw. Tools Technol. Transfer **21**(1), 1–29 (2017). https://doi.org/10.1007/s10009-017-0469-y
2. Bhadra, T., Paul, S.: Weed management in sugar beet: A review. Fundam. Appli. Agricult. **5**, 1 (2020)
3. Canziani, A., Paszke, A., Culurciello, E.: An analysis of deep neural network models for practical applications. CoRR abs/ arXiv: 1605.07678 (2016)
4. Cioni, F., Maines, G.: Weed Control in Sugarbeet. Sugar Tech. **12**(3–4), 243–255 (2010)
5. DeChant, C., Han, S., Lipson, H.: Predicting the accuracy of neural networks from final and intermediate layer outputs. In: ICML 2019 Workshop on Identifying and Understanding Deep Learning Phenomena (2019)
6. Frasconi, C., et al.: Design and full realization of physical weed control (PWC) automated machine within the RHEA project. In: Second International Conference on Robotics and associated High-technologies and Equipment for Agriculture and forestry (RHEA-2014)- New trends in mobile robotics, perception and actuation for agriculture and forestry, May 21–23 2014, Madrid, Spain New trends in mobile robotics, perception and actuation for agriculture and forestry, pp. 3–11 (2014)
7. Gao, J., French, A.P., Pound, M.P., He, Y., Pridmore, T.P., Pieters, J.G.: Deep convolutional neural networks for image-based Convolvulus sepium detection in sugar beet fields. Plant Meth. **16**(1), 29 (2020)
8. Giselsson, T., Jørgensen, R., Jensen, P., Dyrmann, M., Midtiby, H.: A public image database for benchmark of plant seedling classification algorithms. arXiv: Computer Vision and Pattern Recognition (Dec 2017)
9. Glaroudis, D., Iossifides, A., Chatzimisios, P.: Survey, comparison and research challenges of IoT application protocols for smart farming. Comput. Netw. **168**, 107037 (2020)
10. Hendrycks, D., Dietterich, T.: Benchmarking neural network robustness to common corruptions and perturbations. In: International Conference on Learning Representations (2019)
11. Hooker, S., Erhan, D., Kindermans, P.J., Kim, B.: A benchmark for interpretability methods in deep neural networks (2019)
12. Howard, J., Gugger, S.: Fastai: A layered api for deep learning. Information **11**(2) (2020)
13. Ignatov, A., et al.: Ai benchmark: All about deep learning on smartphones in 2019. In: 2019 IEEE/CVF International Conference on Computer Vision Workshop (ICCVW), pp. 3617–3635 (2019)

14. Islam, N., Rashid, M.M., Pasandideh, F., Ray, B., Moore, S., Kadel, R.: A review of applications and communication technologies for internet of things (IoT) and unmanned aerial vehicle (UAV) based sustainable smart farming. Sustainability **13**, 1821 (2021)
15. v. Kistowski, J., Arnold, J.A., Huppler, K., Lange, K.D., Henning, J.L., Cao, P.: How to build a benchmark. In: Proceedings of the 6th ACM/SPEC International Conference on Performance Engineering, ICPE 2015, p. 333–336. Association for Computing Machinery, New York (2015)
16. Lottes, P., Hoeferlin, M., Sander, S., Muter, M., Schulze, P., Stachniss, L.C.: An effective classification system for separating sugar beets and weeds for precision farming applications. In: 2016 IEEE International Conference on Robotics and Automation (ICRA), pp. 5157–5163. IEEE, Stockholm, Sweden (May 2016)
17. Lottes, P., Hoeferlin, M., Sander, S., Müter, M., Schulze, P., Stachniss, L.C.: An effective classification system for separating sugar beets and weeds for precision farming applications. In: 2016 IEEE International Conference on Robotics and Automation (ICRA), pp. 5157–5163 (2016)
18. Luo, C., He, X., Zhan, J., Wang, L., Gao, W., Dai, J.: Comparison and benchmarking of ai models and frameworks on mobile devices (2020)
19. Machleb, J., Peteinatos, G.G., Sökefeld, M., Gerhards, R.: Sensor-based intrarow mechanical weed control in sugar beets with motorized finger weeders. Agronomy **11**(8), 1517 (2021)
20. Martin, C.H., Mahoney, M.W.: Implicit self-regularization in deep neural networks: Evidence from random matrix theory and implications for learning. CoRR abs/ arXiv: 1810.01075 (2018)
21. May, M.J.: Economic consequences for UK farmers of growing GM herbicide tolerant sugar beet. Ann. Appli. Biol. **142**, 41–48 (2003)
22. Milioto, A., Lottes, P., Stachniss, C.: Real-time blob-wise sugar beets vs weeds classification for monitoring fields using convolutional neural networks. ISPRS Ann. Photogram. Remote Sens. Spatial Inform. Sci. **4**, 41–48 (2017)
23. Nasirahmadi, A., Wilczek, U., Hensel, O.: Sugar beet damage detection during harvesting using different convolutional neural network models. Agriculture **11**(11) (2021)
24. Perugini, Engeler: Neural network learning time: effects of network and training set size. In: International 1989 Joint Conference on Neural Networks, vol. 2, pp. 395–401 (1989)
25. Raja, R., Nguyen, T.T., Slaughter, D.C., Fennimore, S.A.: Real-time robotic weed knife control system for tomato and lettuce based on geometric appearance of plant labels. Biosys. Eng. **194**, 152–164 (2020)
26. Ramirez, W., Achanccaray, P., Mendoza, L.F., Pacheco, M.A.C.: deep convolutional neural networks for weed detection in agricultural crops using optical aerial images. In: The International Archives of the Photogrammetry, Remote Sensing and Spatial Information Sciences XLII-3/W12-2020, pp. 551–555 (Nov 2020)
27. Reddi, V.J., et al.. Mlperf inference benchmark. In: 2020 ACM/IEEE 47th Annual International Symposium on Computer Architecture (ISCA), pp. 446–459 (2020)
28. Russakovsky, O., et al.: ImageNet large scale visual recognition challenge. Int. J. Comput. Vision **115**(3), 211–252 (2015). https://doi.org/10.1007/s11263-015-0816-y
29. Schweizer, E., Dexter, A.: Weed control in sugarbeets (Beta vulgaris) in North America. Rev. Weed Sci. **3**, 113–133 (1987)

126     L. Brodo et al.

30. Suh, H.K., IJsselmuiden, J., Hofstee, J.W., van Henten, E.J.: Transfer learning for the classification of sugar beet and volunteer potato under field conditions. Biosystems Eng. **174**, 50–65 (2018)
31. Unterthiner, T., Keysers, D., Gelly, S., Bousquet, O., Tolstikhin, I.O.: Predicting neural network accuracy from weights. ArXiv abs/ arXiv: 2002.11448 (2020)
32. Wägemann, P., Distler, T., Eichler, C., Schröder-Preikschat, W.: Benchmark generation for timing analysis. In: 2017 IEEE Real-Time and Embedded Technology and Applications Symposium (RTAS), pp. 319–330 (2017)
33. Yang, R., Tian, H., Kan, J.: Classification of sugar beets based on hyperspectral and extreme learning machine methods. Appli. Eng. Agricul. **34**, 891–897 (2018)
34. Zhu, H., et al.: Benchmarking and analyzing deep neural network training. In: 2018 IEEE International Symposium on Workload Characterization (IISWC), pp. 88–100 (2018)

# Synthetic Data for Machine Learning on Embedded Systems in Precision Agriculture

Olaniyi Bayonle Alao, Kristian Rother(✉), and Stefan Henkler

Hamm-Lippstadt University of Applied Sciences, 59557 Lippstadt, Germany
olaniyi-bayonle.alao@stud.hshl.de,
{kristian.rother,stefan.henkler}@hshl.de

**Abstract.** Embedded systems are used in precision agriculture for data collection via sensors and for the control of actuators such as sprayers based on machine learning models. For plant classification and monitoring, it is easier to collect data of healthy plants than it is to collect data of plants that are infected by various diseases, because they are simply more common. Sufficient data are therefore often lacking for the accurate detection of diseased plants. In this paper, we outline an approach for the generation of synthetic data of infected plants that can be used to train a machine learning model for the classification of sugar beets. We use image augmentation techniques to build a pipeline that can automatically overlay diseased areas on healthy areas of leaf images.

**Keywords:** Embedded Systems · Machine Learning · Precision Agriculture · Synthetic Data

## 1 Motivation

Agriculture performs a crucial role in food security and the economic infrastructure of a country [15]. However, the agricultural sector requires a considerable amount of land and water and it also poses a substantial threat to the biological variety and variability of life on earth [5,7]. Additionally, in order to achieve better environmental protection of water and soils, there is a need for the reduction of fertilisers and pesticides in crop production [13].

Sugar beets and sugar cane are the two vital plants that supply the raw materials needed for the commercial production of sugar [2,4]. However, diseases like cercospora Leaf Spot (CLS), beet yellow virus, ramularia leaf spot, rhizoctonia root and crown rot, and powdery mildew inhibit the growth of sugar beet plants during cultivation [2,14].

This research is supported by a grant from the Ministry of Economic Affairs, Industry, Climate Action and Energy of the State of North Rhine-Westphalia (MWIDE) as part of the 5G-Landwirtschaft-ML project in the context of the program 5G. NRW (01.05.2022–31.12.2024, grant number 005-2108-0039).

Conventional methods of disease detection and classification entail visual inspections by experts and laboratory tests of plant leaves or soil samples [23]. However, they have proven to be tedious, ineffective and time-consuming [11]. Hence, there is a need for the automation of the detection of diseases in sugar beets by applying precision agriculture techniques.

Precision agriculture uses technology to optimise agricultural production through the use of site-specific management. In crop production, this aims at crop-specific nutrient deficiencies and disease monitoring, application of fertiliser or pesticides, prediction of yields and automated counting of crops. Precision agriculture reduces harmful outputs into the environment by applying only the specific amount of fertiliser or pesticides needed by each plant [1]. However, the most significant limiting factor in precision agriculture is the interpretation of collected data from sensors [12] and the availability of adequate datasets.

Machine learning methods have been used in different studies to classify plant diseases using features like texture, type and colour of plant leaf images [2,20]. Nevertheless, there is a lack of diversity in the quality of plant leaf image datasets. Two limiting factors in precision agriculture are the interpretation of collected data from sensors [12] and the availability of adequate datasets.

Because farmers try to keep their plants healthy, one of the challenges when building adequate datasets for the use of machine learning techniques in precision agriculture is the lack of images of non-healthy plants that are infected by various diseases. To solve this problem, we propose a process for generating synthetic datasets of diseased plants by combining images from different datasets.

In the next Section we give an overview of the related work. In Sect. 3, we present our approach of synthesizing non-healthy plant images. An evaluation of our approach is presented in Sect. 4. We conclude our paper with a summary and outlook in Sect. 5.

## 2   Related Work

Different approaches for synthetic image generation for ML have been proposed in the agricultural domain. Ward et al. [22] proposed a method of synthetically generating images of the Arabidopsis plant described in their research to augment existing natural plant datasets. Their synthetic image dataset generation begins with manually tracing a randomly chosen Arabidopsis leaf image in Blender to produce a 3D mesh of an inspiration leaf based on the original leaf image. Then, more 3D leaf images are created by randomly scaling to model leaves of different shapes and sizes. Next, the synthetically generated plant leaves are circularly arranged close to each other at a similar height. Finally, random background, camera and lightning are added to the generated plant leaves, which are then rendered as a 2D synthetic image and corresponding segmentation mask. Their proposed framework success is evidenced by its average accuracy of 90% in leaf segmentation.

Da Silva et al. [18] proposed three methods for generating synthetic defoliation images used in training CNN-based models to estimate soybean leaf defoliation. Their proposed methods remove leaf-belonging pixels in different ways to simulate actual defoliation in a pre-processed image and returns a new defoiled image along with its level of defoliation. The first method simulates defoliation using random sizes of polygons formed in random pixels in the leaf area. The second method makes circles with random radii to remove leaf-belonging pixels in the leaf region. Then, secondary circles with different radii are generated in the circumference of the main circle. The third method is similar to the second method except that the secondary circles are generated within the main circle. They were able to generate 10,000 synthetic defoilation images with each method. Their models were trained only with the synthetically generated images and evaluated using natural images.

Datasets are also synthetically generated in domains other than precision agriculture. For example, Björklund et al. [3] proposed a framework for generating challenging synthetic license plate images to avoid collecting and annotating the thousands of images required to train a CNN. Likewise, Silvano et al. [19] described a combination of techniques to generate large random synthetic images of license plates to supplement their small volumes of available authentic images for training deep learning-based automated license plate recognition systems.

In the field of biomedical image analysis, Svoboda and Ulman [21] generated synthetic static and time-lapse image sequences of fully 3D fluorescence microscopy images showing the motion of objects of various sizes. Han et al. [8] generated synthetic multi-sequence brain Magnetic Resonance images using Generative Adversarial Networks. Prokopenko et al. [16] investigated approaches for generating synthetic Computed Tomography images from actual Magnetic Resonance Imaging data using GANs to enable single-modality radiotherapy planning in clinical oncology.

## 3   Solution

Our approach for the creation of synthetic data uses images of healthy sugar beet seedlings from one dataset and combines those with the diseased areas of corn leaves from another dataset to create synthetic images of diseased sugar beets. We segment the leaf areas of the diseased and healthy plants from their background and then concatenate the extracted diseased areas intelligently on the healthy leaf areas. First, we propose segmenting foreground and background leaf areas by converting the images to their respective Hue Saturation values (HSV) to find the leaves' upper and lower bound values. We then propose using thresholding algorithms to create binary masks of the leaf areas and the background and finally use boolean operations to create the new image. Furthermore, we propose bringing the infected areas of the diseased leaf to the foreground and then masking out healthy areas to become the background. Figure 1 showcases a visual representation of the proposed synthetic dataset creation pipeline. The extracted disease areas on the left side is concatenated with segmented healthy leaf areas of sugar beets to create synthetic disease images. We used Python 3 and OpenCV 2 to implement the synthetic dataset generation. The sugar beet disease detection models were trained using the generated synthetic images and the fast.ai [9] library.

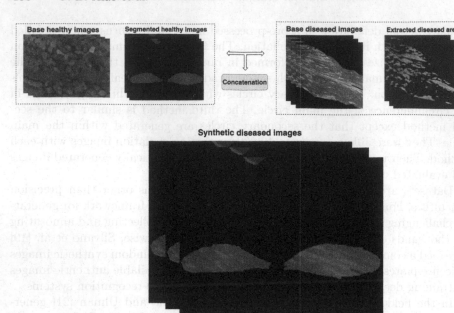

**Fig. 1.** Overview of the proposed approach for generating synthetic data.

## 3.1 Datasets

We used the publicly available PlantVillage [10] and Plant seedlings [6] datasets to generate the synthetic data. The Plant Seedlings dataset contains images of approximately 960 unique plants belonging to 12 species at several growth stages. The dataset was captured at the Aarhus University Flakkebjerg Research station in collaboration with the University of Southern Denmark and Aarhus University. In contrast, the PlantVillage dataset consists of 54,323 images divided into 38 diseased and healthy plants based on 14 different plant species. All images are taken as a single leaf on a solid background labelled only by a class name. For creating the synthetic dataset, we used 463 images of sugar beets from the plant seedlings dataset as a healthy leaf dataset and 513 images of foreground segmented corn leaves infected with grey leaf spot (GLS) in the PlantVillage dataset as the diseased dataset. Corn leaves infected with GLS (caused by cercospora zeae-maydis and cercospora zeina) were used since it was the only disease in the PlantVillage dataset sharing the same genus (cercospora) of CLS which is a common disease for sugar beets caused by cercospora beticola.

## 3.2 Process Overview

The overall process of creating the synthetic dataset consists of four steps. First, the images from different datasets are prepared. Second, the images are segmented. Third, the images are prepared for concatenation and lastly they are concatenated to produce the synthetic images.

**Image Preparation.** Since the used datasets consist of images of different sizes, resizing the images to the same size needs to be done to ensure uniformity in the synthetic dataset. The activity diagram in Fig. 2 shows the complete control flow of operations in preparing the images for image segmentation.

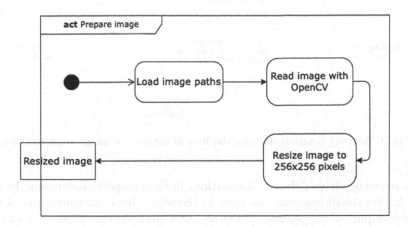

**Fig. 2.** Activity diagram for image preparation.

The images were resized to $256 \times 256$ pixels based on research conducted by Rukundo [17] who found the size works well for training deep learning models. The resized image is passed on to the image segmentation block.

**Image Segmentation.** The leaf areas in images of the diseased and healthy datasets were segmented from their respective backgrounds to reduce the computational complexity of manipulating images with non-uniform backgrounds. Figure 3 shows the flow of actions in segmenting the leaf areas from the background.

First, the resized image is colour transformed from blue-green-red (BGR) into HSV colour space. Using the HSV information of the image, the values of the lower and upper boundary representing the green leaf and disease areas in the image were found by splitting and plotting random pixels in the image into their respective hue and saturation values.

A mask of the leaf area was created with the found lower and upper boundary HSV value using OpenCV *inRange*() function. Then, the masked image was used to create a segmented image from the original image using the *bitwise_AND* operator. Finally, the segmented image was passed on to the next block of actions for further image processing.

**Preparation for Concatenation.** In this section, the actions depicted in Fig. 4 were carried out. The main goal of the actions performed in this section is to rotate the leaf or disease areas in the images vertically. Rotating the leaf/disease area in the vertical direction allows for a consistent positioning of the disease/leaf

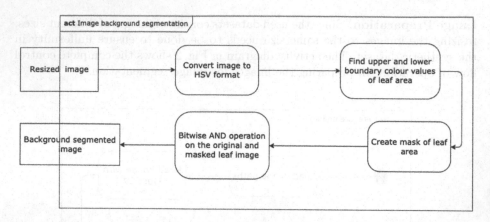

**Fig. 3.** Activity diagram showing the flow of actions for image segmentation.

areas since they have different orientations in their respective datasets. In addition, having the disease and leaf areas in the same direction ensures that a more significant part of the segmented disease area lands on the sugar beet leaf area during image concatenation.

As a first step, the segmented image was converted to grayscale. Converting the image to grayscale reduces the dimension of the image to an 8-bit single-channel image, which allows easier manipulations than BGR images, which hold the information of all three channels. Equation 1 is used for the colour to grayscale algorithm implementation in OpenCV.

$$Y = 0.299R + 0.587G + 0.114B \tag{1}$$

Furthermore, the methods $cv2.ADAPTIVE\_THRESH\_MEAN\_C$ and $cv2.THRESH\_BINARY\_INV$ available in OpenCV were used to create an adaptive threshold binary image of the segmented input image. Binarizing the image enabled us to find the curve joining all the continuous areas along the external boundary of the leaf area since they have the same intensity and colour, i.e. white. Finding the contours of the object of interest in the image gives access to the object's width, height, length, and orientation angle with respect to the whole image.

The values of the contours of the object of interest were then used to calculate the object's width, height, length and orientation angle by drawing a minimum area rectangle around the found leaf area.

Non vertically oriented leaf areas were vertically rotated using wrap affine transformation on the transformation matrix $M$ gotten from the OpenCV function $cv2.getRotationMatrix2D()$. Rotation in OpenCV is counterclockwise (i.e. positive degrees specify counterclockwise rotation while negative degrees specify clockwise rotation). The transformation matrix $M$ is defined by Eq. 2.

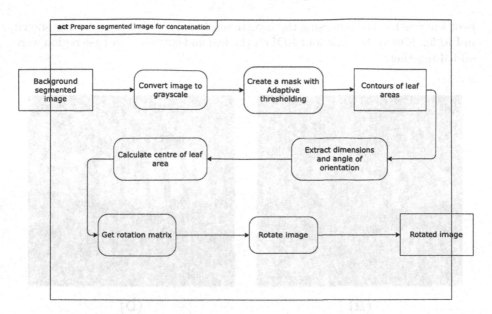

**Fig. 4.** Activity diagram showing the flow of actions for preparing segmented images for concatenation.

$$M = \begin{bmatrix} \alpha & \beta & (1-\alpha).c_x - \beta.c_y \\ -\beta & \alpha & \beta.c_x + (1-\alpha).c_y \end{bmatrix} \tag{2}$$

where $\alpha = scale.\cos\theta$, $\beta = scale.\sin\theta$, $c_x$ and $c_y$ are the x and y coordinates of the centre of the image and *scale* is the isotropic scale factor.

Finally, the vertically rotated image was passed on to the next block for the concatenation operation discussed in the next section.

**Concatenation.** Before concatenating the segmented disease and healthy leaf image, there needs to be a confirmation that the images are of the same dimensions (i.e. $256 \times 256$). Inequality in the size of the images will lead to an error. Figure 6 shows the activity diagram of operations for this section.

A region of interest (ROI) was created on the rotated sugar beet image using the total rows and columns of the disease image. The created ROI has the same size as the disease image. Using the disease image, disease areas only corresponding to the leaf regions were extracted using *bitwise_and* operation as shown in Fig. 5. The bitwise addition decides the pixels to be displayed using an AND operation on each pixel of the images (i.e. a bitwise AND operation is true if and only if both pixels are greater than zero). Next, a mask of the disease was created by converting the diseased image to grayscale and then thresholding the grayscale image using *thresh_binary*. Then an inverse of the mask was created using the *bitwise_not* operation. The inverse mask was used to create areas where the disease will fall on in the leaf area. Then, this region of disease on the sugar beet leaf was blacked out using the inverse mask and *bitwise_operation* as shown in Fig. 5a. Finally, the blackout ROI on the leaf and extracted disease region were added together.

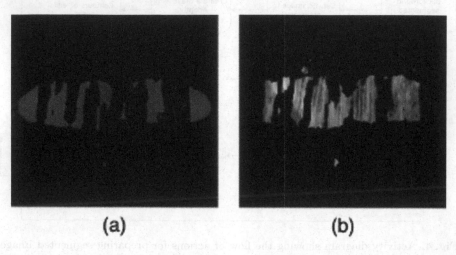

**(a)**                                    **(b)**

**Fig. 5.** (a) Blacked out leaf area for addition of disease (b) Region of disease area which will be overlayed on the leaf area in (a).

### 3.3   Synthetic Dataset

To create the synthetic dataset, every image in the 513 diseased leaf collection was overlaid on the 463 sugar beet images. This resulted in a dataset of 237 520 synthetic images. The generated images are labelled according to their corresponding number in the original image path to easily find the original images used to form the synthetic image. For example, the image with the name *cgls_48_sb_248.png* was generated from the disease image number 48 in corn's grey leaf spot image folder and the sugar beet image number 248.

The pseudo-code for implementing the algorithm for the generation of the synthetic dataset is highlighted in Listing 1.1. The function begins by looping through each disease in the disease dataset path. For each disease, disease areas are segmented and rotated. The function continues by looping through the healthy leaf images which are concatenated with the segmented disease area.

**Listing 1.1.** Pseudo code for generating the synthetic dataset.

```
def createSyntheticImages ():
    for disease in diseasePath:
        open disease
        segment disease
        find orientation
```

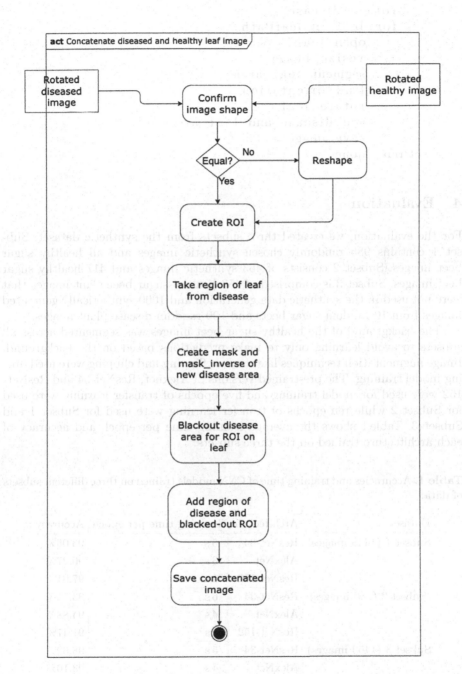

**Fig. 6.** Activity diagram showing the flow of actions for concatenating disease are with leaf area.

```
        rotate disease
        for leaf in leafPath:
            open leaf
            resize image
            segment leaf area
            find orientation
            rotate leaf
            add disease and leaf area
            save image
        return 'done'
```

## 4  Evaluation

For the evaluation, we created three subsets from the synthetic dataset. Subset 1 contains 985 randomly chosen synthetic images and all healthy sugar beet images. Subset 2 consists of 463 synthetic images and 417 healthy sugar beet images. Subset 3 is comprised of 453 healthy sugar beet plant images that were not used in the synthetic data generation and 1000 synthetically generated images from 10 random sugar beets and 100 random disease plant images.

The background of the healthy sugar beet images was segmented across all subsets to avoid learning only to make predictions based on the background. Image augmentation techniques like random flipping and clipping were used during model training. The pre-trained versions of Alexnet, ResNet-34 and ResNet-152 were used for model training and five epochs of transfer learning were used for Subset 2 while ten epochs of transfer learning were used for Subset 1 and Subset 3. Table 1 shows the average training time per epoch and accuracy of each architecture trained on the three subsets.

**Table 1.** Accuracies and training time of CNN models trained on three different subsets of data.

| Dataset | Architecture | Training time per epoch | Accuracy |
|---------|--------------|-------------------------|----------|
| Subset 1 (1448 images) | ResNet-34 | 5 s | 93.05% |
| | AlexNet | 3 s | 90.27% |
| | ResNet-152 | 31 s | 97.91% |
| Subset 2 (880 images) | ResNet-34 | 6 s | 93.75% |
| | AlexNet | 4 s | 94.88% |
| | ResNet-152 | 18 s | 91.47% |
| Subset 3 (1453 images) | ResNet-34 | 5 s | 98.62% |
| | AlexNet | 4 s | 93.10% |
| | ResNet-152 | 15 s | 98.27% |

# 5   Summary and Outlook

In this paper, we outlined a process for the creation of synthetic data of diseased sugar beet seedlings from available datasets of healthy sugar beet seedlings and diseased corn leaves. We evaluated the created data by using it to train different models to differentiate between healthy and diseased sugar beet seedlings. This research is an initial technical feasibility study and can be improved upon in several ways.

On the data level, collecting healthy and diseased images of the target plant would decrease the need for our process. However, it would be interesting to see if a model trained on both synthetic and real images would outperform a model that is only trained on real images.

On a technical level, the process can be improved by having a smoother transfer of the images. This could be achieved by using styleGANs to treat a diseased plant as a different style of a healthy plant.

Another approach for creating the synthetic data is to use image generation from text like DALLE-2 with strings like "Photo of a sugar beet plant with cercospora leaf spot".

Lastly, if one only wants to know if a plant is diseased or not but not which disease the plant has, the issue of no available diseased images could be sidestepped by using techniques that don't require this data such as outlier detection with autoencoders or one-class classifiers.

# References

1. Auernhammer, H.: Precision farming-the environmental challenge. Comput. Electron. Agric. **30**(1–3), 31–43 (2001)
2. Barreto, A., Paulus, S., Varrelmann, M., Mahlein, A.K.: Hyperspectral imaging of symptoms induced by Rhizoctonia Solani in sugar beet: comparison of input data and different machine learning algorithms. J. Plant Dis. Prot. **127**(4), 441–451 (2020)
3. Björklund, T., Fiandrotti, A., Annarumma, M., Francini, G., Magli, E.: Robust license plate recognition using neural networks trained on synthetic images. Pattern Recogn. **93**, 134–146 (2019)
4. Draycott, A.P.: Sugar Beet (2008)
5. Food and Agriculture Organization of the United Nations: The State of Food and Agriculture: Paying Farmers for Environmental Services (2007)
6. Giselsson, T.M., Jørgensen, R.N., Jensen, P.K., Dyrmann, M., Midtiby, H.S.: A public image database for benchmark of plant seedling classification algorithms. arXiv preprint arXiv:1711.05458 (2017)
7. Green, R.E., Cornell, S.J., Scharlemann, J.P., Balmford, A.: Farming and the fate of wild nature. Science **307**(5709), 550–555 (2005)
8. Han, C., et al.: Gan-based synthetic brain MR image generation. In: 2018 IEEE 15th International Symposium on Biomedical Imaging (ISBI 2018), pp. 734–738. IEEE (2018)
9. Howard, J., Gugger, S.: fastai: a layered API for deep learning. Information **11**(2) (2020). https://doi.org/10.3390/info11020108. https://www.mdpi.com/2078-2489/11/2/108

10. Hughes, D., Salathé, M., et al.: An open access repository of images on plant health to enable the development of mobile disease diagnostics. arXiv preprint arXiv:1511.08060 (2015)
11. Lu, J., Tan, L., Jiang, H.: Review on convolutional neural network (CNN) applied to plant leaf disease classification. Agriculture 11(8), 707 (2021)
12. Ondoua, R.N.: Precision agriculture advances and limitations: lessons to the stakeholders (2017)
13. Otero, N., Vitoria, L., Soler, A., Canals, A.: Fertiliser characterisation: major, trace and rare earth elements. Appl. Geochem. 20(8), 1473–1488 (2005)
14. Ozguven, M.M., Adem, K.: Automatic detection and classification of leaf spot disease in sugar beet using deep learning algorithms. Physica A 535, 122537 (2019)
15. Pawlak, K., Kołodziejczak, M.: The role of agriculture in ensuring food security in developing countries: considerations in the context of the problem of sustainable food production. Sustainability 12(13), 5488 (2020)
16. Prokopenko, D., Stadelmann, J.V., Schulz, H., Renisch, S., Dylov, D.V.: Unpaired synthetic image generation in radiology using GANs. In: Nguyen, D., Xing, L., Jiang, S. (eds.) AIRT 2019. LNCS, vol. 11850, pp. 94–101. Springer, Cham (2019). https://doi.org/10.1007/978-3-030-32486-5_12
17. Rukundo, O.: Effects of image size on deep learning. arXiv preprint arXiv:2101.11508 (2021)
18. da Silva, L.A., Bressan, P.O., Gonçalves, D.N., Freitas, D.M., Machado, B.B., Gonçalves, W.N.: Estimating soybean leaf defoliation using convolutional neural networks and synthetic images. Comput. Electron. Agric. 156, 360–368 (2019)
19. Silvano, G., et al.: Synthetic image generation for training deep learning-based automated license plate recognition systems on the brazilian mercosur standard. Des. Autom. Embed. Syst. 25(2), 113–133 (2021)
20. Sujatha, R., Chatterjee, J.M., Jhanjhi, N., Brohi, S.N.: Performance of deep learning vs machine learning in plant leaf disease detection. Microprocess. Microsyst. 80, 103615 (2021)
21. Svoboda, D., Ulman, V.: MitoGen: a framework for generating 3D synthetic time-lapse sequences of cell populations in fluorescence microscopy. IEEE Trans. Med. Imaging 36(1), 310–321 (2016)
22. Ward, D., Moghadam, P., Hudson, N.: Deep leaf segmentation using synthetic data. arXiv preprint arXiv:1807.10931 (2018)
23. Yang, R., Tian, H., Kan, J.: Classification of sugar beets based on hyperspectral and extreme learning machine methods. Appl. Eng. Agric. 34(6), 891–897 (2018)

# Using Network Architecture Search for Optimizing Tensor Compression

Arunachalam Thirunavukkarasu$^{(\boxtimes)}$ and Domenik Helms

Deutsches Zentrum für Luft- und Raumfahrt, Linder Höhe, 51147 Köln, Germany
{arunachalam.thirunavukkarasu,domenik.helms}@dlr.de

**Abstract.** In this work we propose to use Network Architecture Search (NAS) for controlling the per layer parameters of a Tensor Compression (TC) algorithm using Tucker decomposition in order to optimize a given convolutional neural network for its parameter count and thus inference performance on embedded systems. TC enables a quick generation of the next instance in the NAS process, avoiding the need for a time consuming full training after each step. We show that this approach is more efficient than conventional NAS and can outperform all TC heuristics reported so far. Nevertheless it is still a very time consuming process, finding a good solution in the vast search of layer-wise TC. We show that, it is possible to reduce the parameter size upto 85% for the cost of 0.1–1% of Top-1 accuracy on our vision processing benchmarks. Further, it is shown that the compressed model occupies just 20% of the original memory size which is required for storing the entire uncompressed model, with an increase in the inference speed of upto 2.5 times without much loss in the performance indicating potential gains for embedded systems.

**Keywords:** Tensor Compression · Embedded systems · Network Architecture Search · Tucker Decomposition · Convolutional Neural Network

## 1 Introduction

Image recognition is one of the key algorithms for advanced driver assistance systems, e.g., for autonomous vehicles which are composed of large neural networks. In order to classify a single image, the original AlexNet requires around 240 MB of memory just to store the weight parameters which are obtained after training the model. Similarly, VGG model requires around 528 MB for storing its weights with 99% of MAC operations coming from convolutional layers [1]. With increasing network size, storage space required to store their parameters also increases. This leads to a larger inference time when such AI models are employed on embedded devices. For cost, energy and reliability reasons, automotive embedded systems offer only reduced computation resources. In order to

This publication was created as part of the research project "KI Delta Learning" (project number: 19A19013K) funded by the Federal Ministry for Economic Affairs and Energy (BMWi) on the basis of a decision by the German Bundestag.

© IFIP International Federation for Information Processing 2023
Published by Springer Nature Switzerland AG 2023
S. Henkler et al. (Eds.): IESS 2022, IFIP AICT 669, pp. 139–150, 2023.
https://doi.org/10.1007/978-3-031-34214-1_12

bridge the gap between the high demand of these AI application and the limited resources of automotive systems, various compression techniques like pruning, quantization, teacher-student reduction [2], and a promising, but rarely used Tensor Compression (TC) techniques are employed.

According to [3], pruning resulted in a nine times parameter reduction for AlexNet and sixteen times parameter reduction for VGG-16 model. Quantization technique reduces the number of bits (corresponding to filter weights) to read from the memory in a convolutional neural network. Recent methods for quantization offer quantization down to 4–5 bit accuracy for most layers (if supported by the hardware) by using different quantization for inputs and activations [4] or per layer [5] or even per kernel [6] with sacrificing less than half a percent in accuracy [7]. The work carried out by [8] shows that another compression technique 'Knowledge distillation' has relatively higher advantages and perform well on network trained on MNIST.

On the other hand, Tensor Compression splits one of the most used building blocks of image recognition networks, the (2 dimensional) convolution into a linear part (tensor multiplication) and a nonlinear post-processing (activation function and optionally pooling). For the linear part, mathematical methods are used to approximate the tensor by a series of much smaller tensors. The most prominent realization for this is the Tucker decomposition [9] - the tensor equivalent to Singular Value Decomposition (SVD). While the Tucker decomposition itself is straight-forward and easily available in mathematical libraries (in python), it needs to be controlled by two parameters (third and fourth rank of the target tensor) for which not many obvious algorithms exist.

Often a machine learning engineer is needed to design the architecture and structure of the artificial neural networks based on the problem description. Neural Architecture Search (NAS) is a better way of automating this process and Microsoft Neural Network Intelligence [10] has produced toolkits for NAS. This paper analyses, how TC can be applied on neural networks and the potential of NAS to determine the compression parameters. It speaks about the importance of Tucker decomposition, and the effect of different rank values on the compressed models. Further, how to best use the NAS functionality for controlling compression parameters (3rd and 4th ranks) and the importance of fine-tuning are investigated. Finally, performance analysis of compression rates vs. accuracy loss, size requirements and inference time are carried out to evaluate the results of TC by comparing against conventional NAS (performing search of filter-count per layer). The entire implementation is done in Keras and Tensorflow in Python and all the experiments are carried out on a high-performance AI server (NVIDIA DGX-1).

## 2   Related Works

This section speaks about Tensor Compression and its current state-of-the-art, followed by the deployment of NAS in finding a smaller network architecture based on per-layer filter search.

## 2.1  Tensor Compression

TC involves decomposing the original tensors into multiple factors and performing mathematical operations on them, especially mode-n multiplications. TC is rarely researched and no work has fully exploited it's potential. Some of the available decomposition algorithms are Singular Value Decomposition, Canonical Parafac, Tensor Train and finally Tucker Decomposition.

**Singular Value Decomposition (SVD)** is valid only for 2D tensors aka matrices. SVD means decomposing (factorization) the original matrix into three different matrices, thereby reducing original number of factors in real matrix. SVD simplifies matrix calculations and improves the algorithm results with less complexity [13].

$$A_{n \times m} = U_{n \times n} \cdot S_{n \times m} \cdot V_{m \times m}^T \tag{1}$$

Equation 1 gives the mathematical expression of SVD where, the matrix U represents the left singular values along its column and $V^T$ represents the right singular values along its row respectively. The middle matrix S contains the singular values with U and V being orthogonal to each other.

## 2.2  Tucker Decomposition

This particular type of decomposition was introduced by Ledyard R Tucker in the year 1966 [9], which is similar to SVD but applied on tensors. Hence, is also called as Higher Order Singular Value Decomposition. TD splits the original 'n' mode (dimension) tensor into 'n' different factor matrices and a compressed version of the original tensor, called core tensor as shown in Fig. 1. TD does not follow the regular matrix multiplications instead, it works on mode multiplication method. A 3-dimensional tensor has 3 modes namely 'x', 'y', 'z' and applying TD to this tensor will yield 3 factor matrices (one factor per mode) followed by a core tensor of 3 dimension. The equation which represents TD for n dimensional tensor is given in Eq. 2.

$$X \approx G \times_1 U^{(1)} \times_2 U^{(2)} \times_3 \dots \times_N U^{(N)} \tag{2}$$

X - Original tensor,
G - Core tensor,
$U^{(1)}, U^{(2)}, ..., U^{(N)}$ - Factor matrices,
$\times_n$ - denotes the n-mode tensor product

Figure 1 shows a schematic representation of TD of a tensor. The original tensor 'T' of dimensions R1 × R2 × R3 are decomposed into a core tensor 'D' of dimensions 'a × b × c' followed by three factor matrices along each direction with the mentioned dimensions. Size of the core can be decided by the users but care must be taken that minimum values of 'a', 'b', and 'c' should be at least 1. Till date, there is no standard way of selecting the optimized ranks which determine the size of the core tensor. Only trial and error methods has been adopted for appropriate rank selection along with some other search heuristics

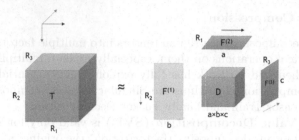

**Fig. 1.** Tucker Decomposition

which exist in theoretical approaches. Tensors of a CNN are 4 dimensional, so applying TD on them needs to be controlled by 4 rank factors namely [a, b, c, d] for [R1, R2, R3, R4].

The compression work by [11] conducted on various models such as AlexNet, VGG-S, VGG-16 etc. were evaluated on a smartphone and Titan X platforms led to a conclusion that the average runtime was enhanced by 2.72 times for AlexNet, by 3.68 times for VGG-S and 3.34 times for VGG-16 networks respectively. It also reported a factor of 1.4 to 3.7 reduction on inference time on embedded hardware for the cost of 0.2–1.7% accuracy. The GitHub implementation [15] which gives an overall idea of how to implement a Canonical & Parafac decomposition along with Tucker decomposition is used a reference for this paper work. Best to our knowledge, the most sophisiticated TC heuristic is discussed in [14], reducing the number of operations on a neural network by a factor of 2–4 for below 0.2% accuracy loss. This is done by a hierarchical rank search on layer clusters.

## 2.3   Model Optimization Using NAS

Microsoft's NNI - a tool to handle automated machine learning (AutoML) problems by choosing hyper-parameters (number of filters and layers, learning rate, activation functions, etc). NNI has a set of inbuilt tuning algorithms which searches for the most efficient architecture [10]. Based on the user defined search criteria it performs a number of trainings (trials) with different parameter values and comes up with the most optimal solution. NNI supports a number of ML frameworks and libraries such as Tensorflow, Keras, Pytorch, Scikit-learn etc.

NAS, a toolkit of NNI can be employed to find appropriate hyper-parameters (filter counts, etc.) in each layer of the neural network within the specific range of choice (search space). NAS will try to come up with an optimized architecture based on the defined tuning algorithm. NAS has a set of different in-built tuning algorithms like Gaussian, Random, annealing, etc. User can choose the most suitable tuning algorithm based on their needs. This filter search is a powerful network optimization method employed using NAS. The only disadvantage of filter-NAS is that, every time a new filter value is chosen from the search space, the entire model has to be trained from scratch requiring huge computational time. This in turn makes the system even more expensive.

# 3 Tensor Compression Implementation

We implemented and tested a methodology for applying TC on convolutional layers of neural networks. For that, we started by reading in the Keras graph, describing the neural network and constructed a second similar instance layer by layer. At user constrained levels, we do not copy over the layer and all its trained weights to the new model, but instead split the activation function, extract the weight tensor, apply a Tucker decomposition with user constrained ranks 'c' and 'd' for the channel (R3) and filter (R4) dimensions respectively. R1 and R2 are the kernel 'a' and 'b' sizes respectively and will not be altered by TC. From the resulting three tensors coming out of the TD we set up three sub 2D convolutional layers without an activation function and used the three tensor's values as weights for those three layers. Finally, the original activation function is added to the last of the three layers. The different steps used in the implementation of TC are as follows:

1. The first sub layer will perform a pointwise convolution on the 3rd factor matrix to reduce the number of channels to 'c' dimension.
2. The output of the previous pointwise convolution will be the input to this second layer where a normal convolution is performed on the core tensor with 'c' input channels and 'd' output channels. This becomes the input for the next sub-layer.
3. Final pointwise convolution with 'c' input channels and the original output channel (number of output filters w.r.t layer without compression). Biases and activation functions are also added as this is the last sub-layer.

While applying Tucker algorithm for each convolutional layer, the user has to specify the rank values. In our work, this process is taken care by the NAS as explained in the coming sections. Once the rank values are obtained, the above 3 steps are repeated for all convolutional layer that are subjected to compression. After applying this algorithm for the convolution layers, the new model with compressed layers is fine tuned to compensate for compression losses.

# 4 NAS Setup

As explained in the previous section, Tucker algorithm is applied on convolutional layers, decomposing it into a sequential 3 sub layers. The dimensions of the 3 sub-layers are determined by the 3rd and 4th rank factors. NAS is assigned the task of finding out the best possible rank values from the user defined search space. The different steps involved in implementing TC using NAS are as follows:

The first step is to define a search space which contains the key parameters (rank values) that are to be tuned using the NNI. The range of values/choices are written in JSON format from which specific rank values for each trials are chosen. Second step is to modify the existing Python codes by including NNI commands in them. The final step in implementing a trial run is to write a 'configuration' file in YAML format containing the experiment details (duration, tuners, assessors, etc). Some of the available tuning algorithms which NAS provides are: TPE, Random Tuner, GP Tuner, etc. In our experiments, only Gaussian Process (GP) tuner is considered which is based on the Bayesian optimization techniques.

## 4.1 Evaluation Metric

Microsoft NNI allows the users to define their own target functions based on which NAS will tune for optimal rank values. Since we are interested in smaller model size without degradation in its performance, an evaluation metric is designed such that it combines both, size and accuracy.

$$t = (1 - a) + (p \cdot \alpha) \tag{3}$$

where, t - target function,
a - validation / top-1 accuracy
p - parameter count of the model
$\alpha$ - constant

The main optimization technique is to lower the target function as much as possible. Parameter count of the model is denoted by 'p'. It can be either total parameters in a model or just the parameter count of the layers which are subjected to compression. Based on the value of 'p' the constant '$\alpha$' is chosen. As the parameter count reduces with a significant increase in accuracy (lowering of loss function (1-a)), the entire target function value will be minimized. This target function is written in the python training script and reported to the NNI tuner after each training. Based on the previous value of target function, NAS tuner chooses the rank values for subsequent trials from the search space. User can choose the tuning algorithm based on which the tuners will tune for rank values.

## 5   Evaluation

In order to analyze the potential of TC, different deep neural networks are chosen and the Tucker algorithm is applied on them. Since CNN tensors are 4 dimensional, applying TD on them needs to be controlled by 4 rank values. Excluding the first two ranks which corresponds to kernel sizes, NAS is employed to choose the third and fourth rank parameters. The behavior of NAS and compression is studied on 3 different networks ranging from smaller generic AI up to a larger modified GoogleNet. These experiments are run on a NVIDIA DGX station inside different Docker containers. Since performing these experiments require even more powerful platforms, in order to fit the experiments within the available resources, some modifications are made on the original model architecture such that their performance is not degraded and still they yield a good result even after modification. To better understand the working of Tucker compression, the results are compared against the normal filter-NAS optimization technique as discussed in Sect. 2.3. The inference time and storage size of the best performing compressed models are also analyzed and compared against the uncompressed model demonstrating the potential of TC.

### Evaluation of Generic AI on MNIST

As a first test with reasonable execution times, we set up an ad hoc network consisting of only four convolutional layers (32 filters each) and trained it on the MNIST digits dataset. The output layer with 10 different classes constitutes a total parameter count of around 28000. After complete training (10 epochs) the model produces a validation accuracy of 98.6%. Decomposition is performed on all convolutional layers except the input layer and the third & fourth rank factors are controlled by NAS. The search space for these rank values is limited from [1, 32] where 32 being the highest rank value (because maximum number of filters per layer is only 32) which denotes the full rank decomposition. NAS chooses the rank values for each trial from this search space based on the tuner's suggestion after each trial. Maximum of 4000 trials are performed.

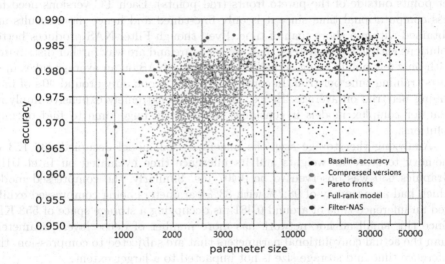

**Fig. 2.** Performance of TC-NAS vs. Filter-NAS for MNIST benchmark (Color figure online)

In the Fig. 2, black point represents the baseline accuracy (uncompressed model), orange points represent the performance of the compressed models at the end of fine-tuning for 3 epochs for different ranks and brown point represents decomposed version for full ranks. Red ones are the pareto points showing a good performance in the tensor compressed models with relatively lower parameter count. Parameter count refers only to convolutional parameters. There were very few points which reported below 95% of accuracy hence they are ignored and plot is clipped from 0.95 to 0.99 along the y-axis. Violet points represents the results of filter-NAS. Pareto points are drawn only for TC-NAS (orange points) and not for filter-NAS (violet points) for this and further analysis discussed in this paper.

As it can be seen from the Fig. 2, there are few models which reports top-1 accuracy of more than 98.5% with significant drop in the parameter count. The most promising compressed model which performs even better than the baseline model accounts for around 12.5% of the parameters being compressed with an increase in 0.17% of accuracy. The next good performing model reports a top-1 accuracy of 98.7%, which is 0.1% more than the baseline model with nearly 83% of the parameters being compressed. Typically, when full ranks (brown point) are applied, it is no longer compressed. In order to compress, the rank values have to be chosen accordingly such that the parameter counts are reduced.

The violet points show the results of 1000 trials (trained for 10 epochs each) of NAS choosing optimal filter counts per convolutional layer. It is observed that NAS on filter tuning seems to perform slightly better for medium to high compression rates (30%–100%). For medium compressions (10%–30%), TC-NAS performs slightly ahead than filter-NAS. For very low compression rates (below 10%), it is clear that NAS on filter tuning is better, hence we have some violet points outside of the pareto fronts (red points). Each TC versions need far less computational time since it is only fine-tuned and hence more results are obtained within a short span of time. Even though Filter-NAS produces better solutions with low parameters, they are very rare and are way further distributed with only few points being actually useful. Filter-NAS on an average takes upto 480 s training time per trial. In contrast, TC-NAS took only around 90 s of fine-tuning per trial on average. Hence, filter-NAS is extremely expensive implying that for complex models it consumes significantly huge time to find optimal solutions.

Analyzing the storage size, the uncompressed model occupied 636 KB of memory to store its weights and its inference time evaluated on Intel UHD Graphics 630 was observed to be 0.407 ms. Similarly, the compressed model which had an accuracy of 98.7% with 83% parameters being compressed exhibited an inference time of around 0.381 ms occupying a storage space of 558 KB. Since this small ad hoc network has more number of dense layer parameters than the actual convolutional parameters that are subjected to compression, the inference time and storage size is not impacted to a larger extent.

## AlexNet on CIFAR-10

AlexNet was first proposed by Alex Krizhevsky, mainly for image classification problems [16] and is usually designed for (224 × 224 × 3) images. Considering our limited resources and timing constraints, our model is made to train on a relatively smaller dataset: CIFAR-10 of dimensions (32, 32, 3). AlexNet has 5 very deep convolutional layers which are subjected to compression except the first input layer. It has a total of around 3.7 million parameters. After training for 100 epochs a top-1 accuracy of 69.01% is achieved (baseline accuracy). Since 89% of the parameters in this model are composed of convolutional layers, we can have a good visualization of compression. A maximum of 4000 trials are made to run on NNI using NAS for tensor compression. Each trial is fine-tuned for 25 epochs consuming 10–12 min on average per trial. In contrast, it took 60 min on average to train the model completely for 100 epochs. The search space is set between [1, 512], depending on the filter counts in each convolutional layer. A scatter plot is drawn between the convolutional parameters count and top-1 accuracy as shown in Fig. 3.

Just like the generic AI analysis, this study is carried out to find the potential of TC against traditional filter-NAS in finding a good optimal solution with low parameter counts. In the Fig. 3 violet points represents the filter-NAS results for 300 trials doing filter search on convolutional layers. Each filter-NAS trial are made to train for 100 full epochs. Due to time constraints, only small number of filter-NAS trials were run (each trial took around 50–60 min even on the very powerful DGX-1 AI accelerator).

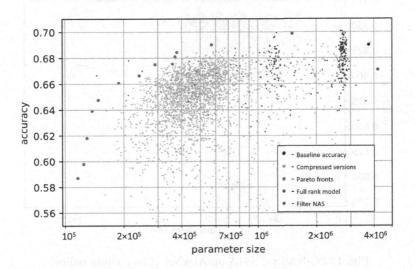

**Fig. 3.** TC-NAS vs. filter-NAS on AlexNet

This analysis can be concluded with the following learnings: for a compression rate of below 10%, clearly NAS on TC is the best choice as it produces good number of pareto points in that range. Also, the filter search approach seems not to produce much versions below 10% of the compression rate. For a range of compression between 10%–25%, again TC-NAS seems to outperform the filter-NAS. It can be seen from the plot as there is a cloud of points in this region produced by compressed versions, leading to more pareto fronts. On the other hand, filter-NAS produces very few points in this region.

The two blue clouds in plot Fig. 3 is due to the NAS trying to learn the optimal rank values. Exploring a particular region of search space, before the tuner moves to other values results in such clouds of points. These clouds will disappear with larger number of trials with significantly high number of performance points. For compression rates from 25% to 50%, filter-NAS seems to dominate slightly producing many optimal solutions and for compression rates of more than 50%, undoubtedly filter-NAS dominates the region. It seems to produce more solutions for greater than 50% of target compression rates.

The uncompressed model occupied a storage space of 16.6 MB with an inference time of 0.847 ms on Intel UHD graphics 630. In order to study the impact of TC on inference time and memory space requirements, one of the best performing tensor compressed models produced by NAS is picked up. The chosen model exhibits a negligible accuracy loss of 0.01% with almost 85% of the convolutional parameters being compressed. The storage space of the compressed model was found to be 3.4 MB, which is just 20% of the size required by the uncompressed model. Its inference time was evaluated to be 0.349 ms indicating that the compressed models are 2.5 times faster than uncompressed versions.

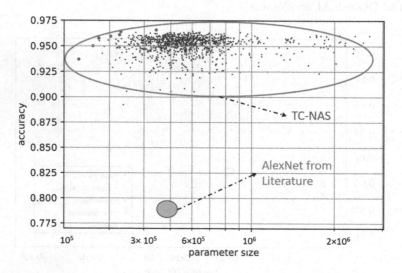

**Fig. 4.** TC-NAS vs. SoTA on AlexNet (Color figure online)

Figure 4 shows the comparison of our work with the current State-of-The Art (SoTA) in Tensor Compression for top-5 accuracy. Yellow circle shows the performance of AlexNet obtained from the work [11] where they have compressed all 5 convolutional layers using TD and VBMF algorithm for rank selection. For a fair analysis, we have drawn a comparison considering the parameters of 2–4 convolutional layers. It can be seen clearly that the top-5 accuracy of TC-NAS exceeds the SoTA. Even though TC-NAS is slower in finiding an optimized model compared the to SoTA, TC-NAS results has the power to provide a cluster of solutions instead of a single one.

## GoogLeNet on MNIST

The original GoogLeNet architecture consists of 9 Inception modules and 2 auxiliary networks and hence it takes significantly larger training time. In order to fit it based on our available resources, the architecture is scaled down such that it is designed to have only 3 inception modules and one auxiliary network and is made to train on the MNIST dataset (tricolor images of dimensions (32, 32, 3)). There are multiple convolutional layers in these inception blocks and almost all of them are subjected to compression in NAS. Hence, the search space relatively

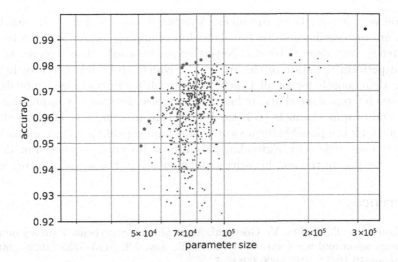

**Fig. 5.** TC-NAS on GoogLeNet

huge taking larger duration to converge. The search space is set between [1, 512], depending on the filter counts in each convolutional layer. After training for 20 epochs, the top-1 accuracy is around 99.4%, which is used as the baseline accuracy for comparison against different compressed versions. The uncompressed version has around 319,960 parameters in total.

Since this model has more than 10 large convolutional layers, despite running around 4000 trials for weeks together, only handful results (~600 trials) could be obtained as shown in Fig. 5. Remaining trials were early stopped by the NAS tuner which it anticipated to have poor performance. Each successfully compressed version took around 20 min on an average for a fine-tune of 3 epochs. Filter-NAS was not performed for this model as it requires complete training for 20 epochs from scratch demanding huge computational resources.

As it can be seen from the Fig. 5, there is a big gap between the black point (baseline) and compressed versions. This gap can be filled if sufficiently more NAS trials are performed. The best performing compressed model had a compression rate of upto 40% with 1% accuracy loss, occupying a memory space of 0.8 MB. On the other hand, the size of the uncompressed model was 5.9 MB. From the analysis, it is evident that TC is capable of producing smaller models with a minimal trade-off for the performance.

## 6   Conclusion

Although, NAS is a very resource demanding optimization technique, combination with TC can speed up its performance by a factor of 4, reducing the need for full training. Because of high computational load, it is hard to fully evaluate the potential of TC-NAS on reasonable benchmarks - even after a month of GPU time on very recent 100k€ machines. Another drawback is that the number of layers are increased when Tucker algorithm is applied, which may be an issue for already very deep networks. Nevertheless, we could clearly show, that we can outperform the state of the art in TC, which, to be fair executes in hours rather than month for small benchmarks resulting in optimized models with increased inference speed and reduced storage size. Instead of compressing both input and output channels (R3 and R4), trying to compress only one channel with one rank is a possible future work. This paper speaks about compression on sequential networks only. Extending this approach to non-sequential models are challenging due to the non-linearities and they are in the scope of future works.

# References

1. Choudhary, T., Mishra, V., Goswami, A., et al.: A comprehensive survey on model compression and acceleration. Artif. Intell. Rev. **53**, 5113–5155 (2020). https://doi.org/10.1007/s10462-020-09816-7
2. Helms, D., Amende, K., Bukhari, S., et al.: Optimizing neural networks for embedded hardware. In: SMACD/PRIME 2021; International Conference on SMACD and 16th Conference on PRIME, pp. 1–6 (2021)
3. Han, S., Mao, H., Dally, W:J.: Deep compression: compressing deep neural networks with pruning, trained quantization and Huffman coding. Published as a Conference Paper at ICLR (oral) (2016). https://doi.org/10.48550/ARXIV.1510.00149
4. Zhou, S., et al.: DoReFa-Net: training low bitwidth convolutional neural networks with low bitwidth gradients, CoRR; abs/1606.06160
5. Uhlich, S., et al.: Mixed precision DNNs: all you need is a good parametrization. arXiv:1905.11452 (2019)
6. Yang, L., Jin, Q.: FracBits: mixed precision quantization via fractional bit-widths. arXiv:2007.02017 (2020)
7. Esser, SK., et al.: Learned step size quantization, CoRR. arXiv:1902.08153 (2019)
8. Hinton, G., Vinyals, O., Dean, J.: Distilling the knowledge in a neural network (2015). arXiv:1503.02531
9. Tucker, LR.: Some mathematical notes on three-mode factor analysis. Psychometrika **31**, 279–311 (1966). https://doi.org/10.1007/bf02289464
10. Microsoft NNI (2021). https://nni.readthedocs.io/en/stable/index.html
11. Kim, Y.-D., Park, E., Yoo, S., et al.: Compression of deep convolutional neural networks for fast and low power mobile applications (2016)
12. Cao, X., Rabusseau, G.: Tensor regression networks with various low-rank tensor approximations (2018). arXiv:1712.09520v2
13. Alter, O., Brown, P.O., Botstein, D.: Singular value decomposition for genome-wide expression data processing and modeling. Proc. Nat. Acad. Sci. (2000). https://www.pnas.org/content/97/18/10101
14. Kim, H., Khan, M.U.K., et al.: Efficient neural network compression. arXiv:1811.12781
15. Accelerating Deep Neural Networks with Tensor Decompositions. https://jacobgil.github.io/deeplearning/tensor-decompositions-deep-learning
16. Krizhevsky, A., Sutskever, I., Hinton, G.E.: Advances in Neural Information Processing Systems. 2nd edn. Curran Associates, Inc. (2012). https://dl.acm.org/doi/10.5555/2999134.2999257

# Author Index

**A**
Alao, Olaniyi Bayonle    127
Arasteh, Emad    101

**B**
Brodo, Luca    115

**C**
Carro, Luigi    53, 89

**D**
Daroui, Arya    65
de Lima, João Paulo C.    89
de Moura, Rafael Fão    89
Dömer, Rainer    65, 101

**F**
Farley, Jackson    78

**G**
Gerstlauer, Andreas    78
Govindasamy, Vivek    101

**H**
Helms, Domenik    139
Henkler, Stefan    115, 127
Herber, Paula    16

**M**
Moura, Rafael Fão de    53
Muoka, Pascal    28

**O**
Obermaisser, Roman    28
Oliveira, Rodrigo S. C.    3
Onwuchekwa, Daniel    28

**R**
Renaux, Douglas B.    3
Rettberg, Achim    41
Rother, Kristian    115, 127

**S**
Schoppmeier, Marcel    16
Steinmetz, Charles    41
Sulak, Adam    41

**T**
Thirunavukkarasu, Arunachalam    139

**U**
Umuomo, Oghenemaro    28

**W**
Wang, Yutong    65
Wehrmeister, Marco A.    3

© IFIP International Federation for Information Processing 2023
Published by Springer Nature Switzerland AG 2023
S. Henkler et al. (Eds.): IESS 2022, IFIP AICT 669, p. 151, 2023.
https://doi.org/10.1007/978-3-031-34214-1

Printed in the United States
by Baker & Taylor Publisher Services